THE COMPLETE SHORT STORIES OF NATALIA GINZBURG

The Complete Short Stories
of Natalia Ginzburg

Translated by
Paul Lewis

UNIVERSITY OF TORONTO PRESS
Toronto   Buffalo   London

© University of Toronto Press Incorporated 2011
Toronto Buffalo London
www.utppublishing.com
Printed in Canada

ISBN 978-0-8020-9920-4

Printed on acid-free, 100% post-consumer recycled paper with
vegetable-based inks.
Toronto Italian Studies

Library and Archives Canada Cataloguing in Publication

Ginzburg, Natalia
The complete short stories of Natalia Ginzburg / translated by Paul Lewis.

(Toronto Italian studies series)
Includes bibliographical references.
ISBN 978-0-8020-9920-4

1. Ginzburg, Natalia – Translations into English.
I. Lewis, Paul, 1981–   II. Title.   III. Series: Toronto Italian studies

PQ4817.I5A2 2011   853'.912   C2010-906444-5

Un'assenza, *Casa al mare*, *Mio Marito*, and *La Madre* are translated with
the permission of the originating publisher, Giulio Einaudi Editore.

This book has been published with the assistance of grants from
the Istituto Italiano di Cultura, Toronto and the European Jewish
Publication Society. The European Jewish Publication Society gives
grants to support the publication of books relevant to Jewish
literature, history, religion, philosophy, politics, and culture.

University of Toronto Press acknowledges the financial assistance to
its publishing program of the Canada Council for the Arts and the
Ontario Arts Council.

 Canada Council Conseil des Arts   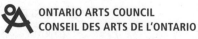 ONTARIO ARTS COUNCIL
for the Arts du Canada   CONSEIL DES ARTS DE L'ONTARIO

University of Toronto Press acknowledges the financial support of
the Government of Canada through the Canada Book Fund for its
publishing activities.

Contents

Acknowledgments

I wish to extend my thanks to Alan Bullock, Emeritus Professor of Italian at the University of Leeds, for his kind permission to quote extensively from his seminal work *Natalia Ginzburg: Human Relationships in a Changing World* (Berg Publishing, 1991) in the introduction which accompanies the translated stories contained in this book. Thanks also go to A. & C. Black Publishers Ltd (on behalf of Berg) for their permission to reproduce passages from Professor Bullock's work.

Where I have quoted from published translations of Ginzburg's essays in the introduction this is indicated by way of an endnote. Otherwise all the translations contained in the introduction and the translation of the stories themselves are of my own undertaking.

I am grateful to Jen Wienstein, Faculty Lecturer at McGill University, and Alan Bullock, Emeritus Professor of Italian at the University of Leeds, for their help and encouragement throughout this project. I would also like to thank Dr Elena Lombardi of the Department of Italian at the University of Bristol and Jennifer Lorch, formerly of the Department of Italian at the University of Warwick, for their helpful suggestions in relation to the translated stories contained in this book. My thanks also go to Ron Schoeffel of the University of Toronto Press for doing so much to help coordinate this project, and finally the Istituto Italiano di Cultura in Toronto and the European Jewish Publication Society for helping to commission this work.

THE COMPLETE SHORT STORIES OF NATALIA GINZBURG

Introduction

Natalia Ginzburg is today recognized as one of the foremost women writers to emerge from twentieth-century Italian literature. Born in 1916 in Palermo under the maiden name of Levi, she was the youngest of five children brought up in a mixed marriage – her father being Jewish and her mother a Catholic. When Ginzburg was aged just three the Levi family left Sicily to resettle in the north of Italy after her father took up a professorship at the University of Turin. Ginzburg's first piece of published work, the short story *Un'assenza* ('An Absence') was written at the age of seventeen and was published in the Florentine periodical *Solaria* in 1933. Her final publication, the short play *Il Cormorano* ('The Cormorant'), was written at the age of seventy-five in 1991; she died in the autumn of the same year. Ginzburg's work represents an impressive and varied collection, as her fictional creations come in the form of short stories, novellas, novels, and plays. She also produced a number of translations and essays, the latter being expressions of her ideas and principles on a wide variety of subjects and themes. Her published works, spanning nearly sixty years of a century that witnessed great social change in Europe, are testament both to a prolific career and to Ginzburg's self-declared realization that '[writing] is my vocation, and I will do it until I die.'[1]

Ginzburg's published short stories have never to date appeared in a single collection – either in their original Italian or in English translation. Her complete works, edited by Cesare Garboli, have appeared in Italian as *Opere raccolte e ordinate dall'Autore* (Mondadori, 1986–7); however, this collection, two volumes of which have so far appeared, contains only a selection of the short stories (in fact only half of them). An earlier volume of her work entitled *Cinque romanzi brevi* (Einaudi, 1964) similarly contains only four of the eight stories; furthermore, with the exception of *La madre* ('The Mother'), none of these has so far been published in English translation. Thus while a selection of Ginzburg's novellas, novels, essays, and plays has been available in English translation for a number of years, the short stories still remain largely unknown to English-speaking audiences. In a sense it is not surprising that no attempt has yet been made to gather all of them into a single collection, as it may be said with some truth that, beyond a common literary format, there is little to tie such a collection together. After all, the eight short stories span over thirty years of Ginzburg's life (1933–65), time in which Ginzburg explored a variety of different literary forms, experienced several personal traumas, and also sustained periods of writer's block. Nevertheless, there are, it is submitted, compelling reasons why these short stories should now be assembled as a single collection in English translation.

First and foremost: Ginzburg's earliest published works – that is, those produced between 1933 and 1941 – were composed exclusively in the short story format. These compositions were fundamental to her emergence as a recognized author and, as such, represent an important collection within the context of Ginzburg's wider repertoire of work. The significance of the earliest short stories primarily lies in their exposure of certain key themes and ideas which would come to characterize much of the author's later work; in particular, the stories reveal characters who are leading essentially unhappy and unfulfilled lives in which they experience a deep sense of alienation from the people who surround them. This dissatisfaction frequently leads her characters to the stark realization that 'they exist in a state of total solitude, unable to relate other than superficially and imperfectly to those around them.'[2] As well as highlighting Ginzburg's general preference for melancholic themes, these early short stories make clear that her chief preoccupation within this context was with the difficulties implicit in developing and sustaining meaningful human relationships.

If Ginzburg's earliest works expose the author's characteristic fascination with the essential bleakness of human existence, the stories also highlight the basic stimulus for most of Ginzburg's writing – her sympathy and compassion for the difficulties faced by women in their social milieu. In a society where women still continue to be consigned to positions of inferiority, Ginzburg's achievement is indeed 'to communicate the complex subtleties of female sensibility though the portrayal of fictional characters whose context is almost invariably one of submission or exploitation.'³ Nevertheless, the stories also highlight Ginzburg's corresponding perception that, even with their apparently advantageous position, in reality men often remain equally vulnerable, struggling to fulfil the role demanded of them in a society dominated by masculine values. It is interesting to note that the theme of male inadequacy (appearing in a variety of different forms) remains the central focus in many of her earliest publications. In this light, it seems clear that the overall emphasis of Ginzburg's work, evident both in her earliest publications and her later work, remains the *reciprocal* nature of those responsibilities which govern relationships between the sexes. This sense of mutual reliance is revealingly described by Ginzburg in her essay *I rapporti umani* ('Human Relationships'): 'the opposite sex walk beside us, brush past us in the street, maybe have thoughts and designs on us which we'll never know; they hold in their hands our future and destiny.'⁴

While Ginzburg's earliest publications point to the emergence of key ideas and themes in the author's work, it is equally clear that the complete collection of her short stories (that is, including the works written after 1940) provides an intriguing insight into the development, improvement, and ultimate perfection of the author's trademark literary style. Producing translations of Ginzburg's work is a painstaking and difficult process. Nevertheless it is possible to faithfully convey the powerful simplicity of Ginzburg's narrative style to English-speaking audiences. Sometimes initially mistaken for superficiality, in reality the unfussy and faithful reproduction of individual personality which lies at the heart of Ginzburg's narrative technique provides an extremely effective means of conveying complex truths about the human condition. Ginzburg's earliest fictional creations undoubtedly evince the unmistakable characteristics of this technique – in particular, her clipped style and uncluttered mode of articulation sustained by an invariably detached tone. Comparing and contrasting these early works with her later short stories demonstrates how Ginzburg's trademark narrative technique matured and flourished with the passage of time.

The evolution of Ginzburg's narrative technique is marked primarily by the gradual emergence of two key stylistic traits which serve to counterbalance the deep sense of pessimism which prevails in her earliest works. First and foremost there is the development of a sense of intimacy between the reader and the author's characters. This is as a result of the author's frequent textual allusions which describe 'the minutiae of day-to-day existence,'⁵ that is, 'innumerable items of apparent trivia which are in reality deeply revealing in the light they throw on individual characters.'[6] Alongside this sense of intimacy is the emergence and consolidation of a sense of humour which 'springs both from the fact that characters' attempts to realize themselves and to achieve their own aims are frequently absurd and nonsensical, and from Ginzburg's own awareness that life often juxtaposes the sublime with the ridiculous, reproducing this accordingly.'[7] In terms of her developing narrative technique, Ginzburg's achievement is made all the more impressive by the fact that she was able to resist any temptation to adopt a more ornate or 'scholarly' style.

By assembling all of Ginzburg's published short stories together in a single collection, it becomes easier to appreciate both the origins of her approach to fiction and her development and ultimate realization of a more balanced and effective literary style. This arguably reached its peak with the publication of her penultimate short story *La madre* ('The Mother') in 1958. In the name of encouraging a deeper understanding of Ginzburg's life's work, this complete collection of her short stories aims to complement those other collections and individual works – plays, novellas, novels, and essays – which are already widely available in English (though which, at least in some cases, are in desperate need of more up-to-date translation).

While Ginzburg's first attempts to write came in her early teenage years, it was not until the age of seventeen that she was able to compose what she later called 'the first serious thing I wrote'[8] – the short story *Un'assenza* ('An Absence'). Writing about this decisive step in later years in her essay *Il mio mestiere* ('My Vocation'), Ginzburg was able to reflect on her feelings of elation which accompanied the completion of this story. Most striking, both as a general indication of her new maturity and as a pointer to one of her most characteristic attitudes as an author, is her awareness that the protagonists of a tale are 'neither good nor evil, but funny and a little sad.'[9] This discovery was indeed a defining moment for the young writer: 'it seemed to me that I discovered how people in books should be – funny and at the same time sad.'[10] Overcome with happiness and a feeling that now she could 'write millions of stories,'[11] Ginzburg followed the completion of *Un'assenza* by embarking on a new phase of intense activity, producing a short story every one or two months.[12]

In *Un'assenza*,[13] written in 1933 and published four years later, masculine inadequacy is the central theme. Deliberately inverting traditional sexual stereotypes at a time when they were significantly more rigid than in our own day, Ginzburg examines a loveless marriage of convenience in which the dominant figure is clearly Maurizio's wife Anna, an ambitious woman anxious to establish a position in polite society and openly dismissive of her placid, good-natured husband, who is possessed of enough wealth to make work unnecessary and whom she consequently despises. Maurizio's general passivity and lack of emotional drive have allowed him to dawdle through life un-thinkingly, and he is only made aware of the essential aridity of his existence when his wife leaves him for a trip to San Remo (where he suspects she is meeting a lover), and in the void created by her absence he realizes for the first time that her presence is quite indifferent to him, that their small son is merely a nuisance, and that he is cut off completely from the world of ordinary people, whose inferior lifestyle disgusts him. In a fleeting moment of truth he contemplates killing himself, only to draw back at the chilling thought of mud at the bot-tom of the river. In a supremely ironic finale Ginzburg shows him seeking refuge in that most typical of masculine stereotypes in Latin society: a visit to the local brothel, where, however, he arrives bored and joyless, unable even to summon up basic lust, a fitting conclusion to an apparently simple story which in effect seriously questions basic assumptions about human behaviour. The message is further empha-sized by Ginzburg's focus throughout on the pathetic Maurizio, his self-assured wife only appearing indirectly as he reflects on the inad-equacy of their relationship.[14]

Written one year later, the short story *Giulietta*[15] focuses on a very dif-ferent kind of male. Aldo, leaving behind his rural background, has moved to the city and become a doctor, acquiring more sophisticated habits and now living with a girl, the Giulietta of the title, something he has carefully kept from his family at home. When his younger brother Ferruccio decides to follow in his footsteps and moves to the town in his turn to attend high school, he naturally expects to be put up by Aldo, who is thus obliged to reveal his relationship with the young woman. If it is easy to appreciate his embarrassment at explaining this to someone who is little more than a child and who must now also con-ceal what is clearly – in view of the period and the brothers' background – a shameful secret, Aldo's reactions to this crisis are clearly contempt-ible. Because Aldo is too shy to explain the situation to Ferruccio on the way home, his confusion at seeing how easily his brother and mistress make friends quickly turns to frustration and anger at his inability to make things clear and is equally quickly revealed as springing from a basic deviousness of character. Initially tempted to flee the apartment and leave the two young people to their own devices, he reluctantly returns home after having gone out to buy cigarettes, only to lose his temper at table when Ferruccio naively suggests they all spend Sunday with the family, feeling 'suffocated by unhappiness and resentment'; conscious that his brother is blameless, he inevitably directs the full brunt of his feelings on Giulietta, whom he observes 'with hostility' as they prepare for bed after he has explained things to Ferruccio. The story ends chillingly with Aldo's sudden awareness that her expression resembles that of her mother, an 'old hag in a rest home,' while she touchingly asks him if he is angry with her.[16]

A combination of parental antagonism and maternal insensitivity is at the root of Ginzburg's next short story, *I bambini* ('The Children'),[17] which appeared in the literary review *Solaria* in 1934. The author's feelings of resentment towards her mother, unable or unwilling even to consider her problems, much less to help her resolve them, were balanced by an equally strong conviction that she could expect no help from her father, a well-intentioned but nevertheless socially incompetent despot whose angry moods and ceaseless criticism of his wife and children dominated the family home.[18] In *I bambini* her parents' characteristics are neatly inverted to produce a hen-pecked father, who, when not absent on business, creeps around the house in his slippers seeking refuge from his wife among the pots and pans in the kitchen, and a tyrannical mother who is constantly scolding and punishing her children while declaring she can no longer bear to put up with them. If this inversion is clearly a fictional transposition of Ginzburg's own domestic environment, the story also reproduces – albeit in extreme form – her feelings of bitterness in relation to both her parents' neglect of her true needs, beginning as it does with the short sentence, 'they had always been afraid of her,' and continuing with the equally significant statement, 'Sometimes they would wonder if there were any other children in the world who didn't love their mother.'[19]

This austere and essentially unhappy life changes suddenly and unexpectedly one evening while the children's father is, as usual, away on business, and their mother receives a visit from her brother-in-law, Uncle Bindi. Packed off to bed earlier than usual, and unable to sleep, Giorgio and Emilia decide to amuse themselves by creeping back to the terrace to say goodnight once more to their mother, only to see her being passionately embraced by Bindi before eventually persuading him to leave. When she realizes they have seen everything, her first panic-stricken reaction is to berate them, but the build-up of conflicting emotions is too much for her and she collapses in tears, at which point the children gather round her and she embraces them fitfully, telling them it has all been a game and begging them not to mention a word to anyone. The story ends on this note of reconciliation, with the children happily fantasizing about a new loving relationship with their mother. The irony of this situation is not lost on the reader, who, unlike the children, has no difficulty in seeing the hollowness of the happy ending, which leaves open the question of the relationship between the adults while making it clear that the mother's new affection is hardly disinterested. While the emphasis throughout this story is on the two children and their reactions to what they see around them, Ginzburg also has an implicit understanding of their mother, whose rapport with her husband is obviously unsatisfactory and whose isolation for long periods during his absence makes it easier to understand her behaviour, thus introducing alongside the more obvious theme of parental neglect that of marital incompatibility and female loneliness.[20]

Written three years later in 1937, *Casa al mare* ('The House by the Sea')[21] is a more complex story, employing the device of a male narrator who is also one of the protagonists. Summoned by his old friend Walter from his home in the city to a small seaside town, the writer is charged with resolving a domestic crisis involving Walter's relationship with his wife Vilma, a neurotic woman unable to communicate with her husband and infatuated with a middle-aged musician named Vrasti. Initially anxious not to interfere in someone else's affairs, he is nonetheless keen to help, but no counselling of any kind takes place, and instead he soon begins to experience feelings of fulfilment, which gradually acquire a specific focus as he allows himself to fall under Vilma's spell, first unconsciously and then, on realizing what is happening, with increasing inevitability as he attempts to delude himself into thinking that all is well. When he finally decides to depart, Vilma reacts with a tearful scene that predictably degenerates into a passionate embrace, and as he leaves the next morning filled with 'shame' and 'disgust' at what has happened, he is conscious that 'I had resolved nothing, and had indeed made things worse, possibly ruining them forever.' If the narrator's total lack of will power makes him the classic example of masculine indecision, his friend Walter is equally inconclusive, hiding his inability to communicate with his wife under a mask of cold indifference to all that surrounds him; even after learning of his friend's betrayal he reacts only with 'a gesture of helplessness.' The third man in this tale, Vrasti, a scruffy, alcoholic piano player who babbles incoherently in his cups, is a more obvious example of the fundamental impotence affecting both the other male protagonists, which ensures that Vilma's problems continue unchecked. In the end we learn that following the death of her child Vilma has left her husband to live with the musician, confirming the narrator's suspicions that his incompetence has helped destroy this marriage.[22]

It is clear with the benefit of hindsight that the four short stories which appeared during this early period 1933–7, while remarkable in someone not yet clear of her teenage years, were nonetheless as limited, albeit in a different and more subtle way, as Ginzburg's childhood poetry and adventure stories, and destined to lead to a period of writer's block, its main characteristic, as impressed upon her by a painter whose judgment she respected, being their *fortuitousness*, a concept Ginzburg was later able to reflect and elaborate on:

> He said my short stories were not at all badly written, but that they were *fortuitous*, that is to say I knew nothing about reality, and used my imagination, living in an unreal world as do all adolescents; the objects I described and the events I narrated only had the semblance of reality and truth; I had come across them *fortuitously*, fishing haphazardly in a void. I was struck dumb by the truth of these words. I did indeed write *fortuitously*, spying on other people's lives without really understanding them and without knowing anything about them, using my imagination and *pretending to understand*.[23]

This approach, perhaps inevitable in someone of Ginzburg's age, was exaggerated by the author's fierce desire to exclude from her writing anything remotely personal. The result is a series of impressive short stories in which, however, the emphasis is on 'grey, squalid people and things ... a contemptible kind of reality lacking in glory ... an avid, mean desire for little things.'[24] This trend reached its peak with the publication of *Casa al mare*, where the author's excessive focus on the negative qualities of her protagonists results in a set of characters totally credible within their own terms of reference, but, ultimately, lacking in humanity. As Ginzburg became more adept at this kind of writing, turning out 'dry, clear stories ... that came to a convincing conclusion,'[25] she became increasingly aware that her interest in doing so was declining. Nevertheless, it was ostensibly outside events that soon intervened to change the course of her literary output at this time.[26]

In 1938 Ginzburg married the Jewish intellectual Leone Ginzburg, a Marxist whose Jewishness and politics made him a natural target for the attentions of the Fascist police, something that brought her face to face with a state of political conflict she had previously observed from the confines of her family but which now became – quite literally over-night – part of her daily routine. This radical change in her personal circumstances would in itself have been sufficient to turn her attention away from creative composition, and any chance of resolving these problems was further postponed by two successive pregnancies which made it impossible for her to devote any time or energy to something other than the daily care of her children. When in 1940 Italy's declaration of war led to her husband being exiled to the village of Pizzoli in the depressed south, she lost little time in following him, together with their children, and starting a new life in a primitive environment in which the family was required to live on a shoestring with no knowl-edge of when their situation might improve.[27]

An initial rejection of artistic commitment, total and unqualified, to the point where, as she recalls in her essay *Il mio mestiere*, Ginzburg felt only contempt for her work, gradually gave way to feelings of nostal-gia for the joys of writing, memories which, she tells us, often brought her to the verge of tears. Ginzburg's new environment in Pizzoli was one she both loved and hated, a beautiful village set in the country-side, which, however, she had not chosen to inhabit and which was at the same time a source of resentment, peopled by simple country folk who were kind and helpful but with whom she and her husband had nothing in common: urban intellectuals surrounded by primitive peasants. Ironically it was the absence of distractions and of direct political harassment in her lonely village which provided the stimulus for a new period of creativity, inevitably very different from what had gone before.[28]

Written in the spring of 1941, Ginzburg's next short story *Mio marito* ('My Husband')[29] focuses on the powerlessness afflicting the husband of the female narrator, a woman who gradually realizes that her mar-riage to a doctor practising in a depressed southern village is no more than a futile attempt on his part to overcome a sexual obsession with a local peasant girl. The husband's gradual disintegration is skilfully traced in no little detail. Away from the village he is 'incredibly self as-sured' with a 'stern reserved and efficient manner,' but this superficial image vanishes after his return home with his new bride, to whom he soon confesses the truth about their marriage, informing her that the mere sight of his peasant mistress 'stirs something inside me.' This is a moment of truth which, while apparently strengthening the bond between the husband and wife, in reality drives a wedge between them, causing 'something strained' in their dealings with each other which extends to their relationship with the two children she bears him in following years. When one day she catches sight of him on his way to meet Mariuccia in the woods, she realizes: 'He had learned to lie to me, and it didn't bother him any more. My presence in his house had made him worse,' at which point he admits he feels no love for her, especially since Mariuccia is now pregnant. Conscious, however, that he has failed his wife by marrying her under false pretences, he is gradually overcome by shame and increasingly withdraws into silence and solitude, neglecting his appearance, refusing food, and spending sleepless nights alone in his study. When Mariuccia dies in childbirth he is unable to face life without her and shoots himself.[30]

One striking feature of *Mio marito* is the author's focus on the reciprocal nature of the responsibilities which govern relationships between the sexes. Key to understanding this work is the quotation from Saint Paul which appears at the beginning of the story: 'Let every man give his wife what is her due; and let every woman do the same by her husband.'[31] In *Mio marito*, it is clear that neither partner is able to fulfil their respective obligations to each other. The husband is unable to provide his wife with love, having married her for essentially wrong reasons; equally, while the narrator fulfils the traditional wifely role, she utterly fails to communicate with her husband in relation to his emotional needs. Although she is able to exhibit trust, devotion, a sense of duty, and domestic competence, none of this, like her maternity, is enough to help him solve his problem: the spell that binds him to Mariuccia. Albeit undeniably placed from the outset in an impossible situation, it is the narrator's *active* acceptance of the traditional role of inferiority coupled with her inability to respond to her husband's needs, or offer him any sort of positive emotional rapport, that ultimately contributes to his death. As the husband tells her bluntly, 'Your presence ... gives me peace and quiet, but that's all,' and later equally revealingly, 'You're nothing new for me ... You're like my mother and my mother's mother, and all the women who have ever lived in this house.' It is thus apparent that her 'strength' is really only an abundance of patience, which could also be seen as resignation and thus something negative.

Although in some respects this story is entirely consistent with her earlier fictional creations, *Mio marito* is also significant because it marked something of a watershed in Ginzburg's literary career. The doctor suffers from an emotional disorder and demonstrates behaviour which is incompatible with any conventional understanding of normality, an approach that clearly recalls the plots of her earlier tales, particularly *Un'assenza* and *Casa al mare*, which likewise focus on emotional traumas but which, however brilliantly described, do not relate to common experience.[32] Nevertheless it is equally clear that *Mio marito* contains elements of a new style and approach, far more effective than anything that had gone before; most striking in this respect is the author's willingness to draw on her own personal experiences as a direct inspiration in her writing. It is significant that the narrator of *Mio marito* is a woman who, despite being 'as different as possible from myself and my circumstances,'[33] nonetheless has much more in common with Ginzburg than any of her previous literary creations: a woman who moves from a provincial city to the country following her marriage to a rural doctor and whose life thereafter is conditioned by his responsibilities to the village community. If the plot of this tale and its tragic conclusion are indeed very different from the author's life, the background is clearly identical – the minor characters based directly on inhabitants of the area, and, most significantly, the doctor whose destructive passion is at the centre of the story the exact physical replica of the man who treated Ginzburg's children during the three years she spent at Pizzoli.[34]

Four months after completing *Mio marito* and imbued with a new sense of purpose, Ginzburg began work on her first novel: *La strada che va in città* ('The Road to the City'), a work whose title perfectly expresses the contrast between rural and urban environments and, as such, her state of mind, in which the beauty and attraction of her surroundings together with her love-hate relationship with the village were combined with strong feelings of homesickness for Turin. While a detailed analysis of Ginzburg's first novel necessarily goes beyond the scope of this work, it is nevertheless important to recognize that the novel represented a crucial step forward. On one level the book is significant for her ability to fully embrace the notion, hitherto only partially realized in *Mio marito*, that, in order to write successfully, she needed to draw directly on people and things from her everyday life; in addition, however, it also marked the author's realization that she could find an entirely new source of creative inspiration by drawing on memories of her friends and relatives, using them alongside her day-to-day personal experiences. The discovery of this crucial relationship between memory and imagination in her writing led Ginzburg to feel that she could now approach her subjects with a greater degree of humanity and that, as a consequence, she was no longer writing 'fortuitously.'[35]

The collapse of the Fascist regime in July 1943 once again saw outside events intervene and radically change the direction of the Ginzburgs' life, as Italy's surrender in September 1943 and the subsequent occupation by her former ally, Germany, created a situation in which they found themselves deeply involved. Hopes raised by the fall of Mussolini's Fascist rule two months previously and the all-too-brief flowering of political activity in the interim were quickly dashed and replaced by the harshness of martial law and renewed anti-Semitic persecution. Her husband's arrest in Rome, where he had moved in July and where she soon joined him, her virtual destitution following his death in prison after torture, and her need to go into hiding to escape arrest and deportation, all ensured that she had more than her fair share of fear and suffering, rapidly achieving a spirit of maturity in a short space of time. Her return to the capital after its liberation by the Allied troops in June 1944 and employment with the publishing house of Einaudi, first in Rome and later in their head office in Turin, while ultimately signalling the beginning of a return to normality, in reality proved only the beginning of a long process of readjustment among the hardships of daily life in a country torn apart by war and civil strife and in which poverty and squalor were the norm.[36]

One month after the official German surrender in 1945 the cultural review *Mercurio* published Ginzburg's next work entitled *Passaggio di tedeschi a Erra* ('German Soldiers Pass through Erra').[37] This short story describes in chilling detail how the euphoria occasioned by the 1943 armistice in a small rural community gives way to apprehension as the countryside swarms with occupying German forces and the villagers gradually realize that for them the war is not yet over. When one of the local peasants shoots a drunken soldier, disaster is inevitable, and seven inhabitants are executed as a reprisal, including – by mistake – the only person who can speak German and who has throughout acted as interpreter, a striking example of black humour sharper than anything so far produced by the author. With the benefit of hindsight this tale can be seen as a prelude to Ginzburg's third novel *Tutti i nostri ieri* ('All Our Yesterdays'), written seven years later, but is clearly in the first instance dictated by the possibility of speaking freely after so long about the harrowing events she had lived through, and, as such, outside the more conventional range of inspirational subjects.

Notwithstanding this, the familiar theme of male inadequacy remains central. The men in the village are conscious of their status as virile males but are unable to realize it because of the circumstances: occupation by a superior force. There is much empty gesturing: the foolish attempt to stop the trucks, which fails miserably; the lone Communist riding back and forth claiming to have won the war when the armistice is announced; Bissecolo showing off his knowledge of German. Meanwhile the 'professional men' – the local *carabinieri* force – are revealed as being equally impotent when confronted with a superior force, and their shame is compounded by their having to remove their uniforms. The eventual slaughter of the villagers is the direct result of the most foolish of all the instances of masculine thoughtlessness: Antonio Trabanda's long-standing desire to kill a German, something 'he thought about... all the time with a mania which bordered on obsession,' an action which while apparently brave and virile is in reality stupid and catastrophic in its results.[38]

Ginzburg's first attempts to write narrative fiction in peacetime – a time when she felt 'totally defenceless and miserable'[39] – resulted in her second novel entitled È stato così ('The Dry Heart'), which appeared in 1947. The protagonist is the epitome of naive innocence brutalized by misfortune: a young woman whose inability to defend herself against the blows of life leads her first to murder and then to suicide. When seen in context it is clear that it remains a work in which the author has drawn too freely and too deeply on the anguish of past memories to create a character with whom she has a rapport. Two years after completing the work, Ginzburg was able to reflect on its shortcomings: 'When we are happy our imagination is stronger; when we are unhappy our memory works with greater vitality. Suffering makes the imagination weak and lazy.'[40] The effect of this over-reliance on memory is aptly described by Ginzburg: 'It is difficult for us to turn our eyes away from our own life and our own state ... [and] so memories of our own past constantly crop up in the things we write,' causing a 'sympathy which grows up between us and the characters we invent ... tender and almost maternal, warm and damp with tears, intimately physical and stifling.'[41]

If elements of self-indulgence in È stato così are understandable given the author's gloomy state of mind during the immediate postwar period, the novel was nonetheless important in helping Ginzburg to realize the degree to which a writer's personal acquaintance with the facts of life and the range of human experience should influence the process

of creative composition. Her naive faith in the stability of social struc-
tures and her instinctive assumption that happiness, or at least satisfaction, is a recognizable norm in human existence had been swept away
by the war and replaced by an intense awareness of the potential for
unhappiness that exists in the human make-up. This awareness, hark-
ing back to the intuitive feeling that enabled her to focus on distress
in her earliest characters, now allowed her to distinguish consciously
and creatively between feelings of victimization which may dominate
an individual in a specific context and an intellectual realization that
suffering is a fundamental part of the human condition. This valuable
lesson proved, at least in the long term, another important step in
Ginzburg's development as an author. In the two years that elapsed
between the completion of *È stato così* and the composition of her essay
Il mio mestiere she slowly began to adapt to a new life in which some
degree of emotional and spiritual stability could be achieved alongside
a gradual improvement in her material circumstances.[42]

It is clear that her next literary creation, *La madre* ('The Mother'),[43]
evinces a new perception and a new mastery in the author's work.
Composed in 1948 (though not published until 1957), *La madre* is the
description of a family in crisis seen through the eyes of two children,
still young enough to share their mother's bed at night and thus too
naive to understand her emotional problems; though they are sufficient-
ly perceptive to notice everything that happens around them, they inevitably lack the ability to distinguish between trivial details and events
whose importance the reader can recognize as deeply disturbing, thus
ensuring the presence in this story of two distinct levels of reality. Like
the mother in *I bambini*, this similarly unnamed woman also neglects her
children, but in a very different context, apparently more comforting
and supporting but in reality even colder and more isolated. A very
young widow, little more than a child herself, she inhabits a spiritual
void in which the impossibility of establishing fruitful communications
with her children is paralleled by the equally rigid limitations of her
aged parents, who refuse to accept that she still has emotional and sexual needs that cannot be satisfied in the essentially passive role which
society has automatically assigned her on the death of her husband; as a
result she exists in a kind of limbo in which her increasingly desperate
attempts to find some sort of equilibrium emphasize more and more the
difference between her disorganized existence and the solid conventions which regulate the daily life of her family.[44]

Dimly aware that all is not well with their mother, the children marvel at her curious behaviour. Quite clearly, 'their mother was not an important person.' When one day the children see her sitting in a café with a strange man, looking 'relaxed and happy, as she never [looked] when she was at home,' this merely confirms what the reader has known for some time: she has a lover but is prevented by the rigid conventions which govern her position from acknowledging him openly. A trip to Milan by the grandparents to visit some relatives, which coincides with the maid's day off, gives her a chance to invite him home and make friends with the children, who find him charming and are reluctant to go out and play after lunch; when their mother puts them to bed at the end of the day they see nothing strange in her suggestion to avoid mentioning him to their grandparents, who 'did not like receiving guests.' Inevitably this guilty relationship based on subterfuge is doomed to failure, and when she is abandoned by her lover and once more feels alone in the world, she can no longer bear the strain and kills herself, a gesture which elicits no sympathy from the community but merely sanctions the general view that she is a heartless deviant who has abandoned her two children. Shocked by what has happened, the boys try to understand what lies behind their mother's actions, but they are soon distracted, first by the thrilling new life they lead in the country at Aunt Clementina's and, subsequently, on their return home, by the well-regulated routine of life with their grandparents; this sense of security, together with the excitement of growing up, soon leads them to forget their mother and her problems, so that they eventually even forget what she looked like.[45]

La madre represents something of a high point in Ginzburg's literary repertoire – undoubtedly one of her finest works. While the plight of the young female protagonist and the story's conclusion are no less tragic than those evidenced in her earlier works, the narrative technique is far more controlled and perfectly balanced between objective description and personal involvement, well in keeping with the author's definition of successful writing as an amalgam of 'ruthlessness, pride, irony, physical tenderness ... imagination and memory ... clarity and obscurity.'[46] We may see this improvement as indicative of a new lease of life, made manifest two years later by her marriage to Gabriele Baldini, later appointed to the Chair of English in Rome, where Ginzburg subsequently took up residence. A succession of successful novels shows that Ginzburg's creative energies prospered over the next decade: Valentino ('Valentino') in 1951 was followed by Tutti i nostri ieri ('All

Our Yesterdays') the year after and *Sagittario* ('Sagittarius') in 1957. In 1959, her life took a radically different direction when she moved from Rome to London following her husband's appointment there as the Director of the Italian Institute. This new environment proved productive in literary terms as her nostalgia for her past life burst forth in one of her best-known works: *Le voci della sera* ('Voices in the Evening') released in 1961, and the semi-autobiographic novel, *Lessico famigliare* ('Family Sayings') which followed in 1965.[47]

The same year also marked the release of Ginzburg's last published short story, *Il maresciallo* ('The Marshal'),[48] which features a group of children playing in a cellar who are repeatedly visited by a marshal who tells them adventure stories about his life and becomes the focal point of their existence. When they tell an adult about him he no longer comes to see them, and a fight develops when one of their number voices what they all know but dare not mention: he does not exist. Adults break up the fight and close the cellar, thus putting an end to the children's meetings. *Il maresciallo* points to a simple truth: that children need affection and communication. If they don't receive it from adults they create their own surrogate world in which it has a central role, but this cannot last longer than a limited period. As greater maturity develops, this surrogate world is destroyed, causing suffering among the less mature. The story also recalls familiar themes in Ginzburg's earlier short stories – particularly *I bambini* and *La madre* – focusing on the sense of alienation, insecurity, disorientation, and insensitivity which can exist between parents and children. Indeed, while children may make demands on their parents which are sometimes unrealistic, parents must realize this and act as 'fixed points' for their children. If *I bambini* highlights that other areas of an adult's life can make playing this role difficult, or as in *La madre*, impossible, *Il maresciallo* emphasizes the risk of adults who are just too self-absorbed to devote time and attention to their children. Children need a clear framework in which to live their lives; parents and adults generally should be seen as being in charge and thus able to protect and educate their children, as Ginzburg reflected in her essay *Le piccole virtù* ('The Little Virtues'): 'bringing up children essentially means creating a special relationship with them.'[49]

The short stories contained in this volume are the most recent contributions to a growing body of translations which have gradually introduced Ginzburg's fiction to English-speaking audiences. A series of translations published by Carcanet Press (during the 1980s and 1990s) comprises a range of the author's novellas and novels, which include the following publications: 'Lessico famigliare' – *Family Sayings* (1984); 'Tutti i nostri ieri' – *All Our Yesterdays* (1986); 'La città e la casa' – *The City and the House* (1986); 'La famiglia Manzoni' – *The Manzoni Family* (1987); 'Valentino' – *Valentino* (1987); 'Sagittario' – *Sagittarius* (1987); 'La strada che va in città' – *The Road to the City* (1989); 'È stato così' – *The Dry Heart* (1989); 'Famiglia' – *Family* (1992); 'Borghesia' – *Borghesia* (1992). The same publisher has released two further works: *The Things We Used to Say* (1997) (a new translation of *Lessico famigliare*) and *Voices in the Evening* (2003) ('Le voci della sera'). In addition to these publications an interesting miscellany of the author's essays has also appeared: *A Place to Live and Other Selected Essays of Natalia Ginzburg* (Seven Stories Press, 2002). The most recent addition to this body of translated work is an impressive and much-needed complete collection of Ginzburg's plays, which were composed principally between 1965 and 1971. This has appeared under the title *The Wrong Door: The Complete Plays of Natalia Ginzburg* (University of Toronto Press, 2008).

Paul Owen James Lewis, with extensive contributions from Alan Bullock

Notes

1 Natalia Ginzburg, *Il mio mestiere* ('My Vocation'), which appears in her collection of essays entitled *Le piccole virtù* ('The Little Virtues'), reproduced in *Natalia Ginzburg: Opere raccolte e ordinate dall'Autore*, ed. Cesare Garboli (Mondadori, 1986), 1: 840. Henceforth, *NG: Opere*.
2 Alan Bullock, *Natalia Ginzburg: Human Relationships in a Changing World* (Oxford: Berg, 1991), 64.
3 Ibid. 175.
4 Natalia Ginzburg, *I rapporti umani* ('Human Relationships'), which appears in her collection of essays entitled *Le piccole virtù* ('The Little Virtues'), reproduced in *NG, Opere*, 1: 871.
5 Bullock 65.
6 Ibid.
7 Ibid.
8 *NG Opere: Il mio mestiere*, 1: 843.
9 Ibid. 844.
10 Ibid.
11 Ibid.

12 Paragraph derived from Bullock 11–12. See also generally *NG Opere: Il mio mestiere*, 1: 843–5.
13 Natalia Ginzburg, *Un'assenza* ('An Absence') (1933) appears in *NG Opere*, 1: 171–7.
14 Plot summary derived from Bullock 176.
15 Natalia Ginzburg, *Giulietta* (1934) appears in *Solaria*, nos. 5–6 (1934): 66–72. Published under her maiden name Natalia Levi.
16 Plot summary derived from Bullock 176–7.
17 Natalia Ginzburg, *I bambini* ('The Children') (1934) appears in *Solaria*, anno IX, no. 1 (1934): 66–72. Published under her maiden name, Natalia Levi.
18 Paragraph derived from *Bullock, 1991*, 68; on NG's father, Giuseppe Levi, see generally *Bullock, 1991*, 210–11. Giuseppe Levi appears as a character in Ginzburg's semi-autographical novel entitled *Lessico famigliare* ('Family Sayings') reproduced in *NG Opere*, 1: 897–1115.
19 Plot summary derived from Bullock 68–9.
20 Plot summary derived from Bullock 69.
21 Natalia Ginzburg, *Casa al mare* ('The House by the Sea') (1937) appears in *NG Opere*, 1: 178–86.
22 Plot summary derived from Bullock 177–8.
23 Preface to *Cinque romanzi brevi* (Turin: Einaudi, 1964), 6; passage and translation derived from Bullock 14–15.
24 *NG: Opere, Il mio mestiere*, 1: 846; translation derived from Bullock 15.
25 Ibid., 848; translation derived from Bullock 15.
26 Paragraph derived from Bullock 14–15.
27 Paragraph derived from ibid. 16.
28 Paragraph derived from ibid., 16–17. See generally *NG Opere: Il mio mestiere*, 1: 848–50.
29 Natalia Ginzburg, *Mio marito* ('My Husband') (1941) appears in *NG Opere*, 1: 187–202.
30 Plot summary derived from Bullock 178–9.
31 This biblical quotation appears in Latin in NG's original: 'Uxori vir debitum reddat: Similiter autem et uxor viro.' A more orthodox English translation would be: 'Let the husband render unto the wife due benevolence and likewise also the wife unto the husband.'
32 Interpretation and passage derived from Bullock 19.
33 Preface to *Cinque romanzi brevi*, 10; passage cited in Bullock 17.
34 Interpretation and text derived from Bullock 17.
35 Paragraph derived from Bullock 17–19.
36 Paragraph derived from Bullock 20–1.

37 Natalia Ginzburg, *Passaggio di tedeschi a Erra* ('German Soldiers Pass through Erra') (1945) appears in *Mercurio*, anno 2, no. 9 (1945): 35–41.
38 Paragraph derived from Bullock 181.
39 Preface to *Cinque romanzi brevi*, 14; translation derived from Bullock 21.
40 *NG: Il mio mestiere*, 851–2; text and translation derived from Bullock 21–2.
41 Ibid.
42 Paragraph derived from Bullock 22.
43 Natalia Ginzburg, *La madre* ('The Mother') (1948), appears in *NG Opere*, 1: 203–15.
44 Plot summary derived from Bullock 70.
45 Plot summary derived from Bullock 70–1.
46 *NG: Il mio mestiere*, 1: 852, cited in Bullock 22.
47 Paragraph derived from Bullock 22–3.
48 Natalia Ginzburg, *Il maresciallo* ('The Sergeant') appears in *Racconti italiani 1965* (Milano: Selezione dal Reader's Digest 1964), 25–32.
49 Natalia Ginzburg, *Le piccole virtù* reproduced in *NG Opere*, 1: 884.

An Absence

BACK HOME FROM THE STATION he felt lonely in his house; it felt too big for him. Now as never before the long dark curtains, the dusty shelves, and the servant with white cotton gloves who waited on the table seemed meaningless to him. Without Anna, it all took on the appearance of a farce. In the evening the double bed, with its sky-blue satin quilt, made him laugh at first, but then left him feeling miserable. Anna loved things which were lavish, majestic, and old-fashioned. If she had known how to, she would have made herself a dress with drapes and layers, and a wide feather hat as was the fashion once upon a time.

That first evening alone Maurizio went to bed early and slept deeply. In the morning he was woken up by the screams of his child who did not want to have a wash. His eyes began to search for Anna's white bathrobe hanging next to the bed. He could not see it, and then he remembered ... 'Anna is in San Remo.' He thought that he ought to go and scold the child and give him a good talking-to as Anna would have done, tell him, for example, that all good boys wash, and that he would end up like that Pierino Porcospino,[1] and then threaten to take away his new ball. But he realized that he had no desire to do this, so he stayed where he was. After a while the screams stopped and he heard the heavy steps of the nursemaid and her loud voice whispering, "Come along now, go and say good morning to papa." Then the child appeared in front of him at the door with his ruffled blond hair and little red face. "Dear Villi, come here." He helped him climb up onto the bed, stroking his cold little hands with his own, which were covered in sweat. "Who was being naughty a moment ago? You know I don't like naughty children." They played with a ball in their pyjamas for a while and had a great deal of fun. The morning was clear, sunny, and calm. "Now go and get dressed, dear Villi." He spent an hour in the bathtub scrubbing himself all over with the sponge. Then he had a cup of cocoa brought to him. Anna always drank tea, and also had tea brought for him, because, she said, one ought not to give the servants too much to do. 'This isn't a hotel,' she used to say.

He got dressed, went into the study, and stretched out on the settee without taking his shoes off, apologizing in his heart to Anna. 'What on earth shall I do? I don't feel like going out.' He reached out towards the shelf and picked up a volume of modern French poems which Anna

---

1 Popular character from Italian children's stories originally created by Heinrich Hoffman. *Pierino Porcospino* is well known for his wild appearance and mischievous behaviour.

liked. He read one and got bored. He preferred poems with rhymes and rhythm; one day he had said so to Anna, but she had pulled a face.

He tried to imagine Anna in San Remo, and pictured her walking along an avenue in her loose-fitting white coat. He also imagined her, in the evening, wearing her black dress which was cut very low on the back. Anna only dressed in black and white; always black and white, just like the keys on a piano. 'Like this, one is refined,' she used to say. She hated things which were not refined. Sometimes she would describe some of her husband's friends as 'good folk.' But you could tell by the way she said 'good folk' that really she looked down on them.

Sometimes he was not absolutely sure that Anna did not look down on him, and sometimes the thought of having married her filled him with wonder. Before becoming engaged to him she had been courted by a Jewish student for a month; he was a man with a short red beard who spluttered when he spoke. He also knew eleven languages and had many good qualities. Anna had not married him only because she would never deign to marry someone who was ugly and poor. When Anna's parents and Maurizio's father had arranged the marriage, Anna had not refused, and Maurizio had asked himself many times why on earth not. The morning when he first woke up in the large double bed with the sky-blue satin quilt, and Anna next to him, he asked himself if it was really true, and how it could be so. He knew he was very rich, but Anna too was very well off. Anna was not in love with him, and neither was he with Anna. Both of them knew these things, and yet they were not unhappy, even if at the beginning there had been some mild disagreements, because Anna wanted antique furniture while Maurizio liked the twentieth-century style, or because of the tea and the cocoa, and things of that sort.

Maurizio had asked himself many times if Anna was unfaithful to him, and that day he felt certain that she was. He was convinced that she had gone to San Remo to meet a lover and that she would never return from the trip. He imagined a letter from her: 'Maurizio, I can no longer remain silent; our marriage has been a mistake … We must separate.' He pictured her large, clear writing on lilac paper. He imagined Anna's lover, very tall and lean with long curly hair, a Frenchman or maybe a Russian. But no! Anna would come back, she had common sense after all. 'My darling, you can't understand … my child … you don't know what it is to be a mother.' At times she liked to speak like the heroine of a novel: 'I will keep the memory of you as long as I live, of you, and of these beautiful days …'

Then she would return, her hair made lighter by the sea water and those beautiful red lips set against her dark skin, 'Anna, darling Anna!' She would sit in front of him, with her legs crossed and three horizontal furrows would appear on her brow. 'Maurizio, I have something important to say to you.' 'What's the matter?' She would get up, put her hands on his shoulders. Her hands were strong and stained yellow with nicotine. 'Have you looked yet?' 'Looked? What for?' 'A job.' 'Ah ... no, Anna, I forgot.' Then he would begin to remonstrate. 'But, as I see it, there's no hurry. We have plenty of money.' 'That is not the point. It's unseemly for you to remain idle and to take pleasure in it.' The first time that Anna had spoken of finding a job, he had burst out laughing in amazement: 'But a job doing what?' 'Oh Good Lord ... Have you got a Law degree or not?' 'A Law degree? Oh yes, of course.'

Like being married to Anna, having a Law degree amazed him as well. He had put together a very short dissertation, had received low marks across the board, but had still been feted by all and sundry. Notwithstanding this, Anna would readily mention his degree, in polite society, slipping it into any conversation with great skill. 'Yes, when Maurizio graduated ... my father-in-law put on a great luncheon party and invited all his friends ... I went as well. In those days we weren't yet engaged.'

Anna loved memories. One day she had said to Maurizio: 'Tell me a little about your childhood.' Maurizio had been very grateful to her for these words, because he loved memories as well. He had talked at length. His childhood – so memorable, so recent! But Anna had soon got bored as she did not like these memories. In any case, she had imagined the young Maurizio very differently. She had pictured a lively, wilful, and daring boy who climbed trees and ran away from home. Instead ... 'When I was young I always had ear infections and a bandage around my ears. I didn't like playing with the other boys ... I was scared of cows.' He continued, 'Did you know, Anna, that I wore a smock until I was fifteen?' 'What are you talking about? Until you were fifteen?' 'Why yes, Anna, a baggy turquoise smock, with two big pockets.' Anna began laughing, but you could tell she was not pleased. The detail about his smock had not gone down well. 'But really, until you were fifteen?' 'Why yes, Anna ...'

Then there were his playthings. How he longed to talk about his playthings! But Anna wasn't capable of paying attention for any length of time. He used to love beautiful multi-coloured toys – big animals made of cloth or felt and little puppet theatres; mechanical toys did not interest him. He preferred illustrated fairy tales – his dearly loved German fairy tales – and the story of Peter Pan to the books of Jules Verne or Emilio Salgari. None of this pleased Anna. While Anna gave their child sensible and challenging playthings, Maurizio filled his cupboard with old-fashioned toys, simple and expensive ones. He would sometimes come home with three red balloons all at once as they were another old passion of his.

The whole of that day – the one after Anna had left – had passed slowly, smoothly, and vacantly. The evening came, and at dinner time Maurizio and Villi played lots of games: puzzles, painting, and colouring-in, and they stained the carpet with some tomato sauce to the silent disapproval of the servant, Giovanni. Then Maurizio realized that it was late for Villi, and, to make him go to bed without crying, he promised to take him to the cinema on another evening, apologizing in his heart to Anna. The child said goodnight to him. He knelt down to give him a kiss on his little freckled nose, and told him to dream of his mamma. Then he found himself alone at the table, and he discovered for the first time that a dinner table has something sad about it after a meal has finished, covered with the mess of crumbs and peel, half-empty glasses, and creased napkins. He decided to go out.

He found himself in the street with his overcoat unbuttoned, and felt a gentle sense of well-being as the fresh breeze blew on his face. 'Where can I go? To the cinema?' He began walking on the bridge: beneath him ran the river; it was dark, muddy, and flecked with red lights. 'Where can I go?' He stopped to lean against the parapet. 'Anna … Now she will be dancing, and then she will drink champagne, and then … with her lover … My God, why am I not jealous of Anna?' He looked at the sky, the little moon, and the handful of gloomy-looking clouds. He had never believed in God. 'Oh God, if you do exist, make me jealous of Anna, just for a single moment, make me horribly jealous of Anna …' He tried to remember her, her fresh lips, her small breasts, and her soft, endearing hands, 'Anna, Anna!' But there was nothing. Nothing moved in him, no shiver roused him. In the sky, the little moon covered itself with a cloud, as if taunting him. He felt tired, disheartened, and alone. He remembered something Anna had said, half-jokingly, half-seriously, one day while they were bickering: 'There's no blood in your veins, just water.' Water, indeed, not blood; just fresh, clear water. He could not recall ever having suffered from anything or for anyone. He could not recall ever having been in love.

He could not recall ever having fiercely lusted after a woman. The only dreams he remembered were his strange childhood daydreams, mixed up with absurd fairy tales and old legends. All of a sudden he felt he had understood truly what he was. 'God, why didn't you make me a man, like all the other men? Why don't you give me the strength to protect my child, to stand up for Anna?' He was interrogating God in this way because he needed to pick on someone. 'I'm nothing more than a child, a child just like my own child.' He realized that he was experiencing an all-too-rare moment of awareness. 'I don't even love Villi really. I have fun with him and his toys. But if we were to become poor tomorrow, I wouldn't have the energy to look for a job for his sake. Who am I useful to, who would suffer if I ... if I were to disappear ...' People came and went around him, but by this time he thought of nothing else but himself and the river. 'If I were to throw myself off ... Anna would receive a telegram: "Tragic accident – return at once." How frightened she would be! She would think of Villi. Then in the paper: "Cut off in his prime, grieving relatives announce the death of ..." But I couldn't throw myself into the river. It's so dark and dirty, full of all of the city's rubbish. Anna says that I am squeamish.' "I couldn't be a lawyer, Anna, poor people disgust me." "But you don't have to put their clothes on, for goodness' sake! They're your clients ... You just speak to them about the case." "I know Anna, but the smell of garlic and onion upsets me." Sometimes he would exaggerate just to get on Anna's nerves.

Little by little he moved away from the parapet. He began walking again. The moon reappeared: a clear, cold light spread across his heart. Very slowly he began to feel himself again. 'And why shouldn't I go ... to see that nice little blonde girl ... Mimi, Lili or whatever her name is?' He walked with a firmer and quicker stride. He felt vaguely proud of having briefly thought of suicide a moment before on the bridge. 'Cici, Lili – what the hell is her name? That nice little blonde girl who has dimples like Villi.' Who could tell how Villi would turn out when he grew up? Like him, or like Anna? Anna had been a gossipy and precocious child, she had entered early into society, where she had learned to flirt with a grace and refinement which characterized everything she did. Even as a child she had travelled a lot, and she knew how to handle people. He did not. At fifteen he had been a skinny boy who wore a baggy turquoise smock and had no interest in women ... He slipped down a dark alley, lit by a gas lamp. 'Now then my darling Anna. You are in San Remo with your lover and I am here with my pretty Titi or Cici, or whatever her name is. Here I am.'

He climbed the few steps, and casually rang the bell, wiping his feet scrupulously on the mat. When they came to open the door he went in without any hurry, apologizing in his heart to Anna.

Giulietta

HE'D HAD TO WAIT FOR a good while under the station portico. Two porters in blue jackets were eating apples near him; a core fell right by his feet and he watched it turn brown, and then a sparrow flew down to peck at it. 'Lord God' – he moaned to himself – 'that boy, how am I going to explain to him ... explain to him about Giulietta? Straightaway, before we get home, I'll say to him: "I need to speak to you man to man. You have to understand, I was unhappy living by myself ... Get married? No, no, it's not about that ..."' He had taken her into his house a year ago, Giulietta that is, but he had never spoken of this in letters to his relatives, or during his short visits home. He spotted his brother from a distance, among the other people who were arriving; 'he's still in mourning' he thought, looking down remorsefully at his own yellow shoes.

"Ferruccio my dear brother, how are you?" he said, kissing him on the cheek. Ferruccio swung on his arm in a playful way. Aldo lived in the suburbs, and during the long journey home on the tram, he didn't stop talking for a moment. "I'm so happy about starting high school! It was hard work to convince mamma though. 'You'll be all alone in the city ... if only there were schools nearby where we live,' she said. 'But Aldo's in the city,' I said to her. 'Aldo has studied, so why shouldn't I study and become a doctor as well?' You earn a lot, don't you? You're so well dressed! I wanted to come out of mourning as well, but mamma wouldn't have it. She still cries, you know, when she speaks about poor papa. I've brought some jelly sweets, here, do you want one?" He pulled out a packet from his pocket. "The blue ones are the best, but you prefer mints, don't you? Oh, I'm so happy to finally be at high school! I'll need to study a little at the start, in order to prove myself. This year we'll be doing the *Inferno*, isn't that right?" "Yes, Dante, the *Inferno*," Aldo repeated rather distractedly. 'The *Inferno* ... Lord God, how can I explain to him? He's just a boy ... I haven't seen him for such a long time, I thought that he would have grown up. "Ferruccio, I need to speak to you man to man ..." How ridiculous, he doesn't even come up to my shoulders.' The jelly sweets had left him with an unpleasant bittersweet aftertaste. 'All that talk of family bonds. What have we got in common, me and this little boy with black socks? What nonsense!'

While they were climbing the stairs up to the house, Aldo said, "Ferruccio, don't go thinking that my house is anything special. Four rooms – a little flat, that's all. I earn very little. Here we are; don't ring, I have the key." He showed him into the hall, and made him put down his case. "Now come, I'll show you to your room. Here; it's not big, but

it's comfortable, and from the window you can see the mountains."
Ferruccio looked out of the window: below there was an area with a
little grass which looked parched and dry: lots of children were playing
around a pile of stones; the women sitting together on the ground were
sewing, some had taken off their shoes; further in the distance there
was a house under construction, balconies which had been painted red,
and an area for playing bowls. "On Sunday I can go and play bowls,"
said Ferruccio happily. "I love bowling." From the room nearby there
came the sound of a sewing machine. Ferruccio asked, "Who's in that
room? The maid?", Then Aldo, in a loud and nonchalant way, called
out, "Giulietta, Giulietta." The machine stopped, and Giulietta appeared at the door: she was wearing a dress with large green and yellow
flowers, made of the same material that is sometimes used to cover
armchairs. "Hello," she said to Ferruccio, while brushing away the
pieces of white thread from her dress. "I hope you've had a good journey. Aldo, what are you waiting for to introduce me? Your brother always has his head in the clouds."

Aldo was standing in the middle of the room: his hands were hot
and felt heavy and he didn't know what to do with them. "I'm sorry,
I forgot … Signorina Giulietta Fanti … my brother Ferruccio." "Very
pleased to meet you," said Ferruccio, who seemed a little taken aback.
"Signorina, please, could I interest you at all in one of these jelly sweets.
I think the blue ones are the best." "Thank you, how kind, but really I
don't know if I could … one of these blue ones, did you say? Could I
have an orange one too? Thank you, how kind you are. Can I help you
unpack?" Giulietta skipped from one piece of furniture to the next: her
tiny bottom, her breasts, and the curls behind the nape of her neck
bobbed up and down as she went. Her face was sweaty and red from
enthusiasm. "Well well, a high school student! I would have liked to
have studied too, if it weren't for my circumstances … you know how
it is when you're hard up! I could have done really well, I even won a
prize in the fourth year of primary school." Aldo went into the hall, and
took his hat down from the hat-stand. "I'm just popping downstairs a
moment to buy some cigarettes," he said as he left. On his way to the
tobacconist he thought to himself without much conviction, 'When all's
said and done, I'm a free man; in my house I do as I please. Ferruccio
can think whatever he likes, write whatever he wants to mamma: Aldo
is living with a … and if mamma wants to come and fetch him, they can
all go to hell.'

He felt tempted not to return to the house, but rather to rush off blindly into the dark night of the city and follow an unknown woman down an unknown street. He could slip away and leave Ferruccio and Giulietta together to get on with things. On returning, he found them sitting at the table for supper, in the little dining room. "You know what," cried Giulietta, "your brother and I are getting on really well; we have a lot in common; he even likes spicy sauce, like me."

The maid, a girl with a dazed expression, went back and forth from the kitchen. During the supper Aldo didn't say a word, and devoured all the bread that he could lay his hands on, while Giulietta watched him with reproachful eyes. "One evening back home," said Ferruccio, "I got completely drunk. 'Hey everybody,' I said, 'I'm the king of the world, I'm the king of the world!' What a racket we made! It was such fun." In his suitcase, they had found some nuts, as well as little jars of jam and honey. Giulietta asked for permission to open one straight- away: "Thank you, thank you so much; I bet it's delicious. If only my dear little mother were here, don't you think Aldo? She would be so happy. She's seventy-two, and only has one tooth left, isn't that true Aldo? But how greedy she is!"

"The nuts come from our tree," Ferruccio explained. "Do you re- member Aldo, the one in front of the house. You should see the amount of fruit in our little garden, Signorina Giulietta. Apricots and great big prunes the size of my head. And the pears? Don't even talk about the pears!"

"How beautiful the countryside must be," Giulietta sighed. "I've never been." "You've never been, really?" said Ferruccio, who was very taken with Giulietta. "Well then, one Sunday we must bring her home with us; what do you say Aldo? Mamma would be happy to meet her." "Oh, you are so kind, thank you. I would like that so much, I mean, to meet your dear mamma." Aldo got up from the table abruptly, throw- ing his napkin to the ground, and went out onto the balcony. "This is unbearable," he muttered to himself, "unbearable." He felt himself be- ing suffocated by unhappiness and resentment. 'And the best bit is that I feel like an intruder; they're chatting away like old friends. They have so much in common; they even both like spicy sauce.'

He went back in to drink the coffee, and Giulietta came to sit on his knees. "Aldo, you are naughty," she said in an affected voice, ruffling the tuft of hair on his forehead. "Do you know that my legs are covered in bruises? You always kick me during the night."

Ferruccio was already in bed and about to go to sleep when Aldo came into his room. "I wanted to say goodnight to you, Ferruccio. I wanted to tell you that I'm happy to have you here, in my house." Sitting on the edge of the bed, he stroked his hair. "I also wanted to ask you … if you do write to mamma, there's no need to speak of … of Signorina Giulietta. Try to understand me dear brother; she's a nice girl, and she keeps the house in order, and does the linen. She loves me. She is alone in the world: she has nothing but her mother, an old hag who lives in a rest home: she goes to see her every Saturday. She kept me company when I was lonely … Anyway, as I was saying, she's a nice girl."

"I understand," said Ferruccio, winking in a knowing way. "Do you sleep together in the same bed? You're lucky, she's pretty. You've done well, you've done very well; I envy you. I'm the same, you know. One evening a friend of mine wanted to take me to see a woman, he already knew her. But then it started raining so we stayed at home and played cards."

"I like your brother," said Giulietta as she got undressed. Aldo was observing her with hostility. As she lay down next to him, he said to her, "Can you please stop making those silly comments, I mean, all that talk of kicking. It's not true, when have I ever kicked you? You silly girl! And in front of Ferruccio …" "But, let's be honest, your Ferruccio isn't a child anymore, and there are certain things that he should be aware of now." "Yes, yes, but it's none of your business. Leave it to me … there's plenty of time. It's none of your business." They stopped talking: Aldo lay motionless, contemplating the ceiling. "Anyway, it'll be useful to have Ferruccio here; they'll send more money from home." He remembered having a horrible pair of red and violet striped pyjamas, which Giulietta had chosen for him at the market. He turned to look at Giulietta and found that she bore a curious resemblance to her mother, the little old hag in the rest home. "Are you annoyed with me?" she said in a sleepy voice, and he turned out the light.

The Children

THEY HAD ALWAYS BEEN AFRAID of her. Everything that belonged to her – her wooden-heeled babouches, the umbrella with a monkey's head on the handle, the pink packet of peppermints which she kept on her bedside table – all of these things took on a strange and evil meaning in their eyes. In the living room, there was an album of old photographs which they often liked to look at. In these photographs their mother would appear holding them on her lap or sitting next to them on the carpet, joking and smiling. But when had this time been? They couldn't remember. They thought back over their short lives but could only remember being told off and punished. When she told them off, their mother would say, in a despondent way: "You'll be the death of me, I'm tired of you." Her hands were dry and strong, and could hurt very much.

Sometimes they would wonder if there were other children in the world who didn't love their mother. They thought of their friends and characters from books they had read, but decided that they must be the only ones. They tried to invent a new mother; they wanted her to be plump and blonde like the mother of their little friends – the Oppenheims. She would be a fat lady who dressed in bright colours. She would know how to make puddings, tell stories, sing the song of La Cornacchia del Canadà;[1] and in the evenings she would come and tuck them up in their small beds. They would have been happy with a mother like that. Instead they lived the frenetic and difficult life of children who go to school, and whose existence is really quite similar to the grown ups'. In the mornings they would wake early, wash in cold water, and then drink a cup of bitter and runny cocoa. Emilia, who had plaits and didn't know how to comb her hair by herself, had to go to her mother's room to have a fine comb pulled through her hair. Their school was far away, but they weren't allowed to take the tram. If they brought home a 'ten out of ten' in their homework diary their mother would give them fifty centesimi as a reward. They had to put this in their money box so that in the future they could buy new pen nibs and exercise books. 'I don't want them to get into the habit of throwing their money away on sweets, do I?' their mother would say. Their father would agree.

The children saw very little of their father: he was always away on business, and from one time to the next he would forget which form

---

1 *La Cornacchia del Canadà* ('The Canadian Crow') is a traditional rhyming children's song which was particularly popular in Italy during the 1950s.

they were in at school. When he caressed them he would yawn at the same time, and that is how they knew that he had four gold teeth. They would have liked to go out with him, to eat meringues or go to the cinema, but he didn't like going out. Instead he would pad around the house in his plushy slippers and idle about in the kitchen, where he chatted with the cook, lifting the lids off the saucepans and giving his advice. The children realized quite soon that he too was afraid of their mother; even a big man like him with his hairy hands and booming cough was afraid of their mother.

They had dinner in their bathrobes because it was Saturday and every Saturday at seven o'clock they would have a bath. Their father was in London, and that very same day he had sent a postcard which had three cats in a basket on the front. They ate in silence, their pea soup was too salty, and Giorgio was about to say so, until Emilia poked his elbow so that he would keep quiet. Their mother would only have started shrieking at the cook, and then at them. They were so difficult to please, whereas she, when she was a little girl …

That evening their mother was wearing a strange dress which they had never seen before – it was the colour of red wine; she was wearing lipstick as well. After supper their Uncle Bindi came round for coffee.

Uncle Bindi was a younger brother of their father; he wasn't married but he had a little red car which he said was his wife. More than anything else he liked funny things, going to the cinema, and also dogs. He was tall and thin, dressed in grey flannels, and he never wore a waistcoat, not even in winter. "Signora, allow me to kiss your hand," he said, bowing to their mother. "Signorina, allow me to kiss your little hand," he said, bowing to Emilia. He then sat at the table and finished the artichokes that Giorgio had left on his plate; then he snapped off the stalks from the cherries which had come from the fruit bowl, showing that he knew how to tie them with his tongue. Their mother laughed and laughed. Nobody made her laugh like Uncle Bindi did. "My dear, the colour of your dress reminds me of a tie that I once had … what a tie it was … I've left my little girl friend tonight to come and see you. Yes, my little girl friend, she's a pretty little thing, but nothing compares to an evening with you. You've been an angel to call me tonight. Let's go out on the terrace; perhaps you'll let me taste your cherry brandy. Giorgio, my good little fellow, would you like a little sip too?" "Go straight to bed children," said their mother, "and mind that you don't leave the light on."

They slept together in the same room at the end of the corridor; the wash basin was hidden behind a folding screen. On the folding screen there was a scene of swallows and storks chasing each other across a clear green sky. "Emilia," Giorgio asked, "can you help me untie my shoes?" Emilia came out from behind the folding screen in her little skirt and sat down next to him. "You always make knots that you can't undo! Right, there you are. Now you can undo the button that I can't reach at the bottom of my back."

The window opened onto the garden, and the children looked out. Down in the garden lit up by the moon, the grass was dotted with daisies and the magnolia tree had two large white flowers on it. The nude child on the fountain was revealing his little stone behind to the sky. "It would be nice to have a swing in between those two plane trees down there," said Emilia. "The Oppenheims have got one, haven't they? I would like them to come and play in our garden one day." "We must invite them Emilia, we must. Then we can play the game where you put ivy on your head like that time at their house, do you remember? We must tell mamma to call and invite them." "She won't want to call them, you know, or she'll just offer them a snack of coffee, milk, and bread and butter when they don't like coffee and milk." They got undressed and turned off the light; they lay down on little beds which were set well apart – after Emilia's first communion they had been separated – and put their hands together to say a short prayer.

"Emilia, I'm not tired, I can't sleep and she's sent us to bed earlier than usual. Uncle Bindi will get bored all alone with her, and perhaps he'd be glad to see us. Emilia, Emilia, shall we go out on the terrace to see him? He'd laugh and be happy, and mamma wouldn't think of telling us off." "You're crazy! Close your eyes and go to sleep."

"Emilia, I want to say good night to Uncle Bindi and tell him something that I forgot to say to him; it won't take a minute. I want to tell him that this morning at school I was given a prize; I really must tell him." "Mamma will tell us off."

"No, she won't tell us off, she's always in a good mood when Uncle Bindi is around. Don't you remember that day, it was Christmas day and you dropped a glass and she didn't say anything? Uncle Bindi will laugh so much when he sees us come in our nightshirts." Stumbling barefoot, they crossed the dark corridor: the light was turned off in the kitchen as well and the servants had already gone up to the floor above. Giggling uncontrollably the children stopped in front of the velvet screen which separated the corridor from the hallway. In the hallway the light was still on. "Do you really want to go already Bindi?" said their mother. "Yes I must go. Goodbye you lovely creature." The children moved the curtain back a little, and looked on without being seen. Now I'll jump out and shout 'Boo!' thought Giorgio all of a sudden.

Uncle Bindi put on his raincoat and tied a chequered scarf around his neck. "I'll jump out and shout 'Boo!' … Emilia, I'm going to jump out and shout 'Boo!'" whispered Giorgio, but Emilia held him back: "Wait." "Goodbye you lovely creature," Uncle Bindi repeated. Their mother was standing in front of him. All of a sudden he took her by the wrists and pulled her towards him, laughing. They watched him kiss her, and caress her arms; against their mother's slender arms his hands looked monstrously large and red. "A little kiss … another little kiss come on, what's wrong with that?" Their mother had sunk onto his chest; she was pale and they heard her breathing hard. "No Bindi, no," she begged, "go now, please go now." Their uncle moved away from her and opened the door; "Very well, goodbye then"; he smiled and tipped his hat. They heard him run down the stairs, and hurry across the gravel on the garden. Their mother closed the door and wiped her brow. She looked pale and her dress was creased. "Mamma," called Giorgio gently. Their mother gave a start and was suddenly roused. "Mamma." Two white ghosts danced towards her. "Oh my goodness, children, children!" she said breathlessly. Her mouth tightened. "Go to bed, go to bed at once," she said in an anguished voice. She pushed them down the corridor and closed the door so that they were all together in their room. "Go straight to bed, do you understand?" She picked up the clothes the children had left on the floor, folded them up and piled them on a seat. "No more, I can't take any more from you. This is too much – I don't want you in the house any more. I shall send you away to boarding school; when it comes to this, boarding school is the only thing left. I shall tell your father as soon as he comes home. Enough is enough, I've been too soft and now you've exhausted me and I don't want anything more to do with you." The children looked at her bewildered; they had never seen her like this before. As she spoke she swallowed her words, her lips quivered, and she beat her chest. "It's too much, it's too much. You've exhausted me, I'm being punished …"

She turned off the light and went towards the window; the children curled up in silence under their sheets. They looked up through the corner of the window at the dark sky obscured by foliage. Everything seemed new to them in the room lit up by the moon; the swallows and storks on the folding screen, the clothes folded up on the chair. The silence was broken by a raucous sob; their mother was bent over the window sill crying. They called to her quietly, "Mamma." "My God, children, children." She threw herself down on Giorgio's bed and buried her face in the pillow. "You're little and you can't understand … you're little and can't understand … it was just a joke. Emilia, children, I tell you it was all a joke. But you mustn't speak to anybody about it. Not to papa, not to your grandma, and not to any of your friends at school. You mustn't even speak about it to your Uncle Bindi. You mustn't speak to anybody about tonight. Can I trust you? You're big enough to know how to keep a secret now. Give me your word of honour. Uncle Bindi is a joker, you know that! He did it for a joke and I knew that." She tried to smile, but her smile quickly turned into a grimace. "Come here both of you, my dear children. Come here, close to me. I don't have anything but you, nothing else in the world. I won't send you to boarding school, I want you to stay close to me. Tomorrow you don't have to go to school, and we'll spend the day together. You'll see, it'll be wonderful … but you mustn't say anything to anybody." She held them close to her, warming their bare feet in her hands. The children didn't know what to say except, "Mamma, mamma."

Emilia timidly stroked her cheek with her finger. "Emilia, my beautiful child!" She allowed them to kiss her over and over, until they were tired out. They kissed her all over, on her burning, tear-stained face and all down her warm neck which smelled of face powder. They felt her dress, her hair, and the scarab beetle pin that intrigued them so much but which they had never dared to touch. They didn't know what to say except, "Mamma, mamma."

"My children, my dear children! But now go to bed and try to sleep; it must be late now!" On her way out she turned again exclaiming, "it was all a joke!"

They lay alone. "Emilia, don't you think Signor Bonaventura[2] looks just like Uncle Bindi?" He wasn't sure if he really believed it, but wanted to talk about his uncle. "I don't know, I can't remember what Signor Bonaventura looks like; now leave me alone, I'm sleepy."

They closed their eyes. Tomorrow … the good Lord was preparing a beautiful day for them, full of delightful new things. In the morning, their mother would come and wake them, and would help them to

---

2 Signor Bonaventura ('Mr Goodluck') is the Italian comic strip hero created by Sergio Tofano. He appeared for the first time in 1917 in the *Corrierino dei Piccoli* – the children's supplement of the Italian newspaper *Corriere della Sera*. Signor Bonaventura is renowned for beginning each tale penniless but ending up a millionaire.

wash, and would wash them with her special scented soap, just like when they had had the measles. Maybe she would even let them wear their white sailor outfits. In the afternoon they would go out, all three of them together holding hands, and who knew where they would go? Perhaps the cinema? Now their mother really had changed. She kissed them and called them 'my dear children,' and they were allowed to kiss her back and sit on her lap. Maybe one day they would even be allowed to invite the Oppenheims. They would order a cream cake, candied fruit, and many other things from the confectioner; they would lay the big table in the garden and it would be a beautiful day.

What fun it would all be! Then one day, their mother would call them and say, 'You've kept the promise very well; I see that you are two good children, and I want to reward you. Giorgio, I have brought this bicycle for you, and Emilia, for you a little gold watch. There, you see …' They fell asleep, their hearts aching with happiness.

The House by the Sea

I HADN'T SEEN MY FRIEND Walter for many years. He used to write to me sometimes, but his childish letters were full of grammatical mistakes and said very little. I was surprised to learn that he had got married. When I knew him, he showed absolutely no interest in any of the women who happened to cross our paths at that time. His remarkable good looks stirred the hearts of many women, but he scorned and cruelly mocked those girls who fell for him. The other young men of our age didn't have much time for him, and I was his only friend.

About five years after his marriage I received a letter from him asking me to come and see him in a seaside town where he was now living with his wife and child. He vaguely mentioned a problem for which he needed my advice.

At the time, I was living with my mother. I had a little job that didn't pay very well, and, in order to make the trip, I asked my mother for money. She accused me of squandering and of having little regard for her, and we had a small argument. An uncle loaned me the money and I left. It was a hot day at the beginning of the summer. During the journey I thought about my friend Walter, but the joy of seeing him again was tainted by a vague uneasiness, a kind of trepidation or anxiety, which I had always felt when remembering him over the years. It was perhaps the fear that he could in some way disturb or destroy the life that I had been building, setting it alight with desires and memories. I was also curious about his wife. I couldn't imagine what she would be like, or what sort of relationship they had.

I arrived at midday at a stuffy, deserted station that had been freshly repainted. Walter was leaning against the wall waiting for me with his hands in his pockets. He hadn't changed at all. He was wearing a pair of cotton trousers and a white shirt, with short sleeves and an open neck. On his broad, tanned face, a smile appeared, and he ambled over to meet me, proffering his hand. I had known he would greet me like that – no cheerful greetings or embrace – nonetheless, I felt uncomfortable. On the way home, as he carried my suitcase which swung by his side, I began asking him about what sort of problems he was having, and without looking at me he said in a curt voice that they were family difficulties and that it had been Vilma, his wife, who had wanted him to send for me.

We met Vilma as she was returning from a swim with their child. She was a tall woman, a little on the plump side, with dark hair which was still wet and grains of sand on her face. She was wearing a chequered sundress that exposed her knees and holding a woven straw hat and a red oilskin handbag. The child seemed very small to me, but they said he was four years old. He was a tiny little thing, very thin, pale, and pretty, with very curly blond hair that came down to his shoulders.

They lived in a small two-storey villa in front of the beach. A room had been prepared for me on the upper floor; the view was not of the sea, but of the countryside. The whole house was dimly lit and filled with a pleasant smell of wood and peaches. We had lunch on the veranda; the rust-coloured curtains made of heavy cotton swayed in the wind and as they moved they revealed the sparkling blue sea, the sky, and the beach with huts painted in vibrant colours. During lunch the child refused to eat and his mother tried to spoon-feed him, prompting him wearily. Walter kept silent, crumbling his bread and staring straight in front of him. Then, all of a sudden, he became angry and said that the food was disgusting and badly cooked, and that had it been nicer the child would certainly have eaten it. Vilma made no response, other than to sigh and lower her head. The child turned from one to the other with fear in his eyes.

"Family squabbles," Walter said to me once we were alone. "When people don't get along any more it only takes the slightest thing. In any case, there are more important problems now. She seems to have fallen in love." I asked whom with, and he replied vaguely that he was an artist. "A musician," he said with an unpleasant mocking smile.

On the same day that I arrived, Vilma decided to speak to me straightaway. It was the evening and Walter had gone out for a moment. She sat down in front of me and, speaking with a resolute frankness which was distressing to see, began to talk about herself and Walter. She had suffered a lot in their years together: I knew Walter, and this fact shouldn't have surprised me. She said that she had got married when she very young and inexperienced. As I looked at her I tried to guess how old she was, but she didn't appear to me to be very young – if anything I'd say she looked older than Walter. She had unruly black hair and narrow eyes, dark blue and piercing. Despite her long nose and her complexion which had been ruined by age, she seemed to me quite good looking. "And now I have met up again with an old friend … Vrasti. He has a superior and noble spirit, and his first instinct has been to help me and show me kindness. But my feelings for him are pure, and cannot possibly harm my child and Walter." She spoke to me freely and in a trusting way; however, instead of inspiring the same trust in me, this left me feeling embarrassed and troubled. She said that all this was complicated because of money problems and the frail health of their child, who was in need of a very stable family atmosphere.

Later I met Vrasti. I knew that he was in the habit of visiting every day; however he was almost pathologically shy, and once he knew that I was there, at first he avoided coming. He was about fifty years old, had long limp hair streaked with grey, light eyes, and a gaunt lined face. He hardly spoke; he sat next to Vilma and watched her sew, fidgeting with the tassels on his scarf. He would call to the reluctant child, seizing him by the wrist and stroking his hair with his large hand, which had broken, shabby fingernails.

"An artist, a true artist," Vilma said to me aside when Vrasti came for the first time. "But it's difficult to get him to play."

I asked Vrasti to play but he said no, absolutely not, but you could tell that he really wanted to very much. Eventually he sat down at the piano and played Mozart and Schumann at length, crudely and tediously.

Vilma would often invite him to join them for dinner and he would refuse, saying it wasn't possible, but it was clear that he really wanted to accept, and was afraid that she would stop insisting and that he would have to go away. At table he handled the cutlery clumsily and drank a great amount, repeatedly pouring himself wine. After drinking, he would splutter unintelligible phrases and then begin to shake. Walter would turn away from him with a disgusted expression. Next to his wife, Vrasti, and the child, he appeared curiously young and healthy. His tall frame, broad shoulders, strong bare arms, and the simple serenity of his body filled the entire room. Vrasti sat timidly at his side with a guilty smile, hardly daring to address him directly. I, on the other hand, was quickly shown familiarity and friendliness.

I had been there for some time and felt very relaxed, and in good health. The thought of having to leave made me feel miserable. So I wrote to my uncle asking for more money and received slightly less than I had asked for, together with a letter of admonishment. My mother also wrote complaining about my absence, her feelings of loneliness since I had left her, and the job I had abandoned. Thoughts of work, the city, and my mother made me unhappy and I dismissed them. I felt as though I had been there for as long as I could remember. The others never mentioned my leaving, nor did they seem to recall that I had been summoned there in order to give them advice. I'd given no advice and nobody had asked me for any. I had understood that the love Vilma professed for Vrasti was not real, but simply a figment of her imagination. She had attached herself to the only person she thought could help her, but perhaps inside she understood how artificial and false this was and suffered even more as a result.

When I received the money from my uncle, I offered a large part of it to Walter and he accepted. When Vilma learned of this, she thanked me and her eyes filled with tears. She said that I had shown myself to be a true friend to them. "I will never forget it," she said.

I would get up very early in the morning and stand at the window: I could see the green dewy lettuce and the red and yellow flowers in the vegetable garden, the vast expanse of fields, and the distant mountains, covered by a light mist. Then I would go downstairs. The beach was almost deserted, and the sand, still untouched by the sun, was damp and cool. I would see Walter (he would get up even earlier than me) emerge from the water and come and meet me with his light, gentle step. He wore a pair of tight mesh trunks that made him appear naked when seen from a distance. Still wet, he would lie down heavily beside me and run a hand through his fair hair. An American girl from a rich family, who had a cabin not far from ours, had fallen in love with him, and, on seeing him alone, would approach in order to speak to him. He would speak to her in an offhand way and then walk off. He had nicknamed her 'the parrot.' He gave everyone nicknames; Vrasti was either 'old Punch' or 'Doctor Stutters.' He told these nicknames to his child and made him laugh.

Vilma and the child used to come to the beach very late. Walter would lift the child onto his shoulders and carry him into the water, making him laugh and scream with fright. The child absolutely adored him and I could see that this made Vilma jealous.

Quite soon I noticed that something strange was happening to Vilma. She now invited the musician to dinner less often, and, generally speaking, it appeared that she had become indifferent as to whether or not she saw him. Vrasti also noticed it eventually, and I sensed that he worried and suffered because of it. She no longer begged him to play and no longer tried to stop him drinking. On one occasion, while speaking of Vrasti in her presence, Walter said 'Doctor Stutters' and she laughed.

I felt her desire to please me in her every gesture, her every word. If she was walking around the house tidying things, or chasing the child on the beach, or stretching out, I sensed that she was doing it not for Vrasti, but for me.

I should have left straightway. But I couldn't do it. At first, I told myself that I was imagining things. I fooled myself into believing that I had blown things out of proportion. Nonetheless I avoided being alone with her. I spent most of the day wandering round the countryside with Walter.

During our interminable walks he always remained silent. We would watch the sun set while stretched out on a rock cliff, surrounded by wild vegetation of prickly pears and palms that fell vertically into the sea. I had no idea what those intervening years had meant for Walter while we had been far apart, what he had done, believed, longed for, but I knew that to question him would have been useless. He asked me no questions, and I knew that he would take no interest in anything I could have told him. Such a lack of interest in somebody else would have mortified me, yet in him I saw it as totally natural and obvious and felt no pain. I understood, better now than I had in the past, that he was different from other people and estranged from them, and for this reason all his relationships were strange, inexplicable, and offensive to everybody except me. He was like a large, solitary tree. The wind that blew through his foliage and the earth that fed his roots were a part of his existence, nothing more. Thus I felt that what gave him joy or pain did not depend on his fellow men, but on mysterious unknown sources, like the earth or the wind.

At times he would speak to me about his child, and he appeared to care for him a great deal. He said that Vilma was not up to raising a child. She got him up late, she didn't let him stay in the water for long or play in the sun without a hat. "And then, look how she dresses him, and lets his curls grow. He's like an actress's child."

Eventually, I decided to leave. When I told Walter, he expressed neither surprise nor regret. But Vilma looked at me with such a desperate expression that I felt a shudder inside me. I had rarely been the object of a woman's desire and this gave me an obscure sense of pleasure. But immediately I felt ashamed of myself. I had gone there to resolve things and make myself useful in some way, but I had resolved nothing, and had indeed made things worse, possibly ruining them forever. I went up to my room and began to pack. It was night-time; I would leave the following morning. Walter had already gone to bed.

A little later, I heard a light knocking at the door, and Vilma came in. She said she had come to see if I needed any help. I had already finished; it was only a little case, I answered. She sat on the bed and watched me while I dealt with my few objects and books. All of a sudden she began sobbing very quietly. I went to her and held her hands. "No. Why? Why Vilma?" I said to her. She placed her head on my shoulder, drew herself close, and kissed me. I kissed her back. I couldn't help myself. I felt I loved that woman just as she did me, and I covered her body with passionate kisses.

When I awoke the following morning I was so tired that I had trouble getting up. I felt ashamed and disgusted. I got dressed distractedly and went down to meet Walter on the beach. I couldn't leave without telling him what had happened. I didn't ask myself whether mentioning it was a good or a bad thing, I knew only that I couldn't leave without speaking to him. I saw him stretched out on the sand with his arms crossed behind his neck. During the night it had been very windy, and the sea was stormy with great foaming waves breaking on the shore.

When he saw me, he got up. "You look pale," he said to me. We began walking along the beach. Anguish and shame prevented me from speaking. "Why are you so quiet? Look, I know, I know you spent the night with her," he said. I stopped and we looked each other in the face. "Yes, she's told me. She's one of those people who make their life an open book. She can't help herself. But you mustn't think badly of her. She's just a poor wretch, that's all. She doesn't even know herself what she wants any more. And now you too have seen how we are." His voice was spent and bitter. I put my hand on his arm. "But don't suffer because of this," he said to me. "If you could only understand how meaningless I find all this! I don't know what I want either." He made a gesture of helplessness. "I ... I don't know," he said.

Vrasti also came along to say goodbye to me. They had woken up the child and all together they accompanied me to the station. Vilma did not say a word. Her face was pale and wore a bewildered expression.

Aboard the train I looked out to say goodbye: I saw for one last time the child's curly hair blowing in the wind, Vilma, and Vrasti, who was waving his floppy hat at me. Then Walter turned round and began to walk away, with his hands in his pockets, and the others followed him.

For the whole journey I couldn't stop thinking about them. Back in the city, for a long time, I thought of nothing else but them; I felt nothing in common with the people around me. I wrote several letters to Walter, but received no reply. Later I learned from strangers that the child had died, they had separated, and Vilma had gone to live with the musician.

My Husband

Let every man give his wife what is her due:
and every woman do the same by her husband.[1]

(I Corinthians 7:3)

I WAS TWENTY-FIVE YEARS OLD when I got married. I had always wanted to get married but had often thought, with a sort of gloomy resignation, that there was not much prospect of it happening. I was orphaned as a child and lived with an elderly aunt and my sister in the country. Our existence was monotonous; besides keeping the house clean and embroidering large tablecloths which we didn't know what to do with once they were finished, we didn't have much to keep us occupied. Ladies would come to visit us sometimes and we would all talk all day about those tablecloths.

The man who wanted to marry me came to our house by chance. He had come to buy a farm which my aunt owned. I don't know how he came to know about this farm. He was just a local district doctor for a little village out in the country, but he was fairly well off as he had private means. He came in his car, and as it was raining, my aunt told him to stay for lunch. He came a few more times and in the end asked me to marry him. It was pointed out to him that I was not rich, but he said this did not matter.

My husband was thirty-seven years old. He was tall and quite smart, his hair was going a little grey, and he wore gold-rimmed glasses. He had a stern, reserved, and efficient manner; one could recognize in him a man accustomed to prescribing treatments for his patients. He was incredibly self-assured. He liked to stand motionless in a room, his hand resting underneath his jacket collar, silently surveying everything around him.

I had barely spoken to him at all when we got married. He had never kissed me or brought me flowers; indeed he had done none of the things which fiancés usually do. All I knew was that he lived in the country with a rough young male servant and an elderly female one called Felicetta in a very old big house surrounded by a large garden. Whether something in my personality had attracted or interested him or whether he had suddenly fallen in love with me, I had no idea. After we had taken leave of my aunt, he helped me into his car, which was covered in mud, and started to drive. The level road, flanked by trees,

---

1 This biblical quotation appears in Latin in Ginzburg's original text as follows: 'Uxori vir debitum reddat: / Similiter autem et uxor viro.'

would take us to our home. I took the opportunity to study him. I looked at him for a long time with some curiosity, and perhaps even a certain impertinence, my eyes wide open underneath my felt hat. Then he turned towards me and smiled. He squeezed my bare, cold hand and said, "We'll have to get to know each other a little."

We spent our first wedding night in a hotel in a village not very far from our own. We were to continue on the following morning. I went up to the room while my husband took care of the petrol. I took off my hat and looked at myself in the big mirror which reflected everything. I was not beautiful – I knew that – but I did have a bright, lively expression and a tall, pleasant figure in my tailored dress. I felt ready to love that man, if he would only help me. He had to help me. I had to make him do this.

Yet when we left the next day nothing had changed at all. We barely said a word to each other, and nothing happened to suggest there was any kind of understanding between us. As a young girl, I had always thought that an event of the kind we had experienced would transform two people, bring them closer or drive them apart forever. I now knew it was possible for neither of these things to happen. I huddled up, chilled inside my overcoat. I had not become a new person.

We arrived home at midday, and Felicetta was waiting for us at the gate. She was a little hunched woman with grey hair and sly, servile ways. The house, the garden, and Felicetta were just as I had imagined them. In the house nothing looked gloomy as is often the way in old houses. It was roomy and light, with white curtains and cane chairs. Ivy and rose plants climbed on the walls and all along the fence.

Once Felicetta had given me the keys, stealing round the rooms behind me to show me every minute detail, I felt happy and ready to prove to my husband and everybody else that I was competent. I was not an educated woman and perhaps I was not very intelligent, but I did know how to keep a well-organized and orderly house. My aunt had taught me. I would apply myself diligently to this task and, in so doing, show my husband what I was really capable of.

That was how my new life started. My husband would spend the whole day away while I busied myself around the house, took care of lunch, made desserts, and prepared jams; I also liked working in the vegetable garden with the male servant. Though I squabbled with Felicetta, I got on well with the male servant. When he tossed his hair back and winked at me, there was something in his wholesome face which made me smile. Sometimes I would go for long walks in the village and talk to the peasants. I asked them questions, and they asked me questions too. But when I came home in the evenings and sat down next to the majolica stove, I felt lonely; I missed my aunt and sister and wanted to be back with them again. I thought about the time when my sister and I would get ready for bed; I remembered our bed-steads, and the balcony looking over the road where we would sit and relax on Sundays.

One evening I started crying. All of a sudden my husband came in. He was pale and very tired. When he saw my dishevelled hair and tear-stained cheeks, he said to me, "What's the matter?" I stayed silent, my head lowered. He sat next to me and caressed me a little. "Are you sad?" he asked. I nodded. He pressed me to his shoulder. Then all of a sudden he got up and went to lock the door. "I've been wanting to talk to you for a while," he said. "I find it difficult, that's why it's taken me so long. Every day I've thought, 'today will be the day,' and every day I've put it off; it was as if I was tongue-tied, I was scared of you. A woman who gets married is scared of her man, but she doesn't realize how much a man is also scared of a woman; she has no idea how much. There are lots of things I want to talk to you about. If we can talk to each other, get to know each other bit by bit, then perhaps we can love each other, and we'll no longer feel sad. When I saw you for the first time, I thought 'I like this woman, I want to love her, I want her to love me and help me, and I want to be happy with her.' Perhaps it seems strange to you that I should need help, but that's the way it is."

He crumpled the pleats of my skirt in his fingers. "There is a woman in this village whom I have loved very much. It's ridiculous to call her a woman; she's not a woman, she's just a child, nothing but a scruffy little animal. She's the daughter of a local peasant. Two years ago I cured her of a bad bout of pleurisy. She was fifteen at the time. Her family is poor; not just poor but mean too; they have a dozen children and wouldn't dream of buying medicine for her. So I paid for the medicine, and after she got better, I would go and look for her in the woods where she would go to gather wood and I would give her a little money, so that she could buy herself something to eat. At home she had nothing but bread and salted potatoes; she didn't see anything unusual in this – her brothers and sisters, her mother and father, and most of their neighbours all lived like this. If I'd given her mother money, she would have quickly hidden it away in her mattress and wouldn't have bought a thing. But I soon saw that the girl was ashamed of buying things, afraid that her mother would find out what was happening, and

I realized that she too was tempted to hide the money away in her mattress as she had always seen her mother do, even though I told her that if she did not eat properly, she could get ill again and die."

"I started taking food to her myself every day. To begin with she was ashamed to eat in front of me, but she soon got used to it and she would eat and eat, and when she was full she would stretch out in the sun, and we would spend hours like that, just the two of us. I got an extraordinary pleasure from watching her eat – it was what I most looked forward to during my day – and later when I was alone, I would think about what she had eaten and what I would bring her the next day. It was like this that I started making love to her. Whenever I could I would go to the woods and wait for her, and she would come; I didn't even know why she came, whether it was to eat or to make love, or out of fear that I would get angry with her. Oh how I waited for her! When passion is penetrated by pity and remorse you're done for; it becomes an obsession. I would wake up at night and think about what would happen if I made her pregnant and had to marry her, and the idea of having to share the rest of my life with her filled me with horror. Yet at the same time I couldn't bear to imagine her married to another person, in somebody else's house, and the love that I felt for her was unbearable, it took all my strength away. When I saw you I thought that by tying myself to you I would be freeing myself from her, maybe I would forget her because I didn't want her. I didn't want Mariuccia; it was a woman like you that I wanted, a woman like me, who was mature and responsible. I could see something in you that made me think you might forgive me, that you would agree to help me, and so it seemed to me that if I behaved badly with you, it wouldn't matter, because we would learn to love each other, and all this would go away."

"But how will it go away?" I said. "I don't know," he said, "I don't know. Since we got married I don't think of her anymore in the way I did before, and if I see her I say hello calmly, and she laughs and goes all red, and so I tell myself that in a few years I'll see her married to some peasant, weighed down with children and disfigured by hard work. But then something stirs inside me when I meet her, and I want to follow her to the woods again and hear her laugh and speak in her dialect, and watch her while she collects branches for the fire." "I want to meet her," I said. "You must show her to me. Tomorrow we'll go for a walk and you can show her to me when she goes by." It was my first decisive act and it gave me a sense of satisfaction. "But don't you feel bitter towards me?" he asked. I shook my head. I didn't feel bitter. I didn't know what I felt. I was happy and sad at the same time. It was late, and when we went to have dinner we found all the food was cold: but we didn't feel like eating anyway. We went down to the garden. It was dark and we walked for a long time on the grass. He took my arm and said, "I knew you would understand." He woke several times during the night and pulled me close repeating, "You've understood everything!"

When I saw Mariuccia for the first time she was coming back from the fountain, carrying a bucket of water. She was wearing a faded blue dress and black socks and she was stumbling along with a huge pair of men's shoes on her feet. When she saw me red blushes appeared on her dark face, and she spilled a little water on the steps of the house as she turned to look at me. I was so overwhelmed by this meeting that I asked my husband if we could stop, and we sat down on the stone bench in front of the church. However, just at that moment he was called away and I was left there alone. A deep discomfort came over me at the thought that perhaps I would see Mariuccia every day and that I would never be able to walk around those roads freely again. I had believed that the village where I had come to live would become dear to me, that I would belong in every part of it; now it seemed this had been taken away from me forever. And it was true. Every time I went out I would see her, either rinsing her laundry at the fountain or carrying buckets or holding one of her grubby little siblings in her arms. One day her mother, a fat peasant, invited me into their kitchen; Mariuccia stood by the door with her hands tucked into her apron; she gave me the odd sly and inquisitive look and then disappeared. When I got home I would say to my husband, "I saw Mariuccia today." He would ignore me and look the other way until one day he said to me in an irritated voice, "So what if you saw her? It's all in the past, there's no reason to discuss it any more."

In the end, I stopped venturing beyond the confines of our garden. I was pregnant, and I had become big and heavy. I sat in the garden sewing, and everything around me was calm; the plants were rustling and giving out shadows, the male servant hoed the vegetable garden, and Felicetta went back and forth in the kitchen polishing the copper. Sometimes I would think with amazement about the child that would be born. He belonged to two people who had nothing in common, who had nothing to say to each other and who sat beside each other for long periods of time in silence. Since that evening when my husband had spoken about Mariuccia he had stopped trying to come near me and had shut himself off in silence; sometimes when I spoke to him he would look at me in an empty, almost offended kind of way, as if I had disturbed him from some important thought with my ill-chosen words. Then I would tell myself that our relationship needed to change before the arrival of our baby. Otherwise what would the child think of us? But then I would be moved to laughter: as if a little baby would be able to think.

The child was born in August. My sister and aunt came to stay, a party was organized for the christening, and there was a great deal of coming and going in the house. The child slept in his crib next to my bed. He looked quite red, with his fists closed and a patch of dark hair sticking out under his cap. My husband came to see him all the time; he was cheerful and smiling, and spoke about the child to everybody. One afternoon we found ourselves alone. I had lain down on the pillow, wearied and weakened by the heat. He looked at the child and smiled, stroking his hair and ribbons. "I didn't know that you liked children," I said all of a sudden. He gave a start and he turned to me. "I don't like children," he replied, "but I like this one, because he is ours." "Ours?" I said to him. "He's important to you because he is ours, you mean yours and mine? Do I mean something to you then?" "Yes," he said as if lost in thought, and he came to sit on my bed. "When I come home and know that I will find you here, it gives me a feeling of pleasure and warmth." "Then what happens?" I asked quietly, looking him in the eye. "Then, when I'm in front of you, and I want to tell you about what I have done during the day, what I have thought, and I just can't do it, I don't know why. Or maybe I do know why. It's because there is something in my day, in my thoughts, that I have to hide from you, and so I can't talk to you anymore." "What is it?" "It's this," he said, "I've been meeting with Mariuccia in the woods again." "I knew it," I said. "I've known for a long time." He knelt down in front of me and kissed my bare arms. "Help me, I'm begging you," he said. "What am I going to do if you won't help me?" "But how can I possibly help you?" I screamed, pushing him away, and burst into tears. Then my husband picked up Giorgio, kissed him, gave him to me and said, "everything will be easier now, you'll see."

Since I did not have any milk, a wet nurse was summoned from a nearby village. My sister and aunt left us and we went back to our old routine; I got up and went down to the garden and gradually took up my familiar old tasks again. But the house was transformed by the presence of the child; little white nappies hung in the garden and on the terraces, the velvet dress of the wet nurse swished through the corridors, and her singing echoed throughout the rooms. No longer a young woman, she was a rather fat and proud person who liked to talk a lot about the aristocratic houses where she had worked in the past. We had to buy her new embroidered aprons every month or pins for her handkerchief. When my husband came home I would go to meet him at the gate, and we would go up to Giorgio's room together to watch him sleep; after this we would have dinner and I would tell him about how the wet nurse had bickered with Felicetta, and we would talk for a while about the baby, the coming winter, the supply of wood, and I would tell him about a novel I had read and what I thought about it. He would put his arm around my waist and stroke me while I rested my head on his shoulder. Truly the birth of the child had changed our relationship. Nonetheless, I still sometimes felt that there was something strained in our conversations and in his goodness and affection, although I couldn't focus properly on the feeling. The child was growing up; he had started toddling and putting on weight, and I liked watching him, but at times I wondered if I really loved him. At times I didn't feel like climbing the stairs to go to him. It seemed to me that he belonged to other people, to Felicetta or to the wet nurse maybe, but not to me.

One day I learned that Mariuccia's father had died. My husband had said nothing about it to me. I took my coat and went out. It was snowing. The body had been taken away in the morning. Surrounded by their neighbours in their dark kitchen, Mariuccia and her mother held their heads in their hands, rocking back and forth and letting out shrill cries, as is the custom in the country when a close relative dies; the children, dressed in their best clothes, warmed their cold blue hands against the fire. When I went in, Mariuccia stared at me for a moment with her familiar look of amazement, lit up by a sudden animation. But she quickly recovered herself and began mourning again.

She now wore a black shawl when she walked around the village. Meeting her was still very difficult for me. I would return home unhappy: I could still see her dark eyes in front of me, those big white teeth which stuck out over her lips. But I hardly ever thought about her if we did not happen to meet.

The following year I gave birth to another child. It was a boy again, and we called him Luigi. My sister had got married and gone to live in a city far away and my aunt never left her home, so nobody helped me when I gave birth except for my husband. The wet nurse who had fed the first child left and so a new one came – she was a tall and shy girl who got on well with us and stayed even after Luigi had been weaned. My husband was very happy to have the children. When he came home they were the first thing he asked about, and he would run to see them and play with them until it was bedtime. He loved them, and no doubt thought that I loved them too. It was true that I did love them, but not in the way that once upon a time I had thought a mother ought to love her children. There was something subdued inside me when I held them on my lap. They tugged my hair, pulled on my necklace, wanted to search through my little work box, and I would get irritated and call the wet nurse. Sometimes I thought that maybe I was too sad to have the children. 'But why am I sad?' I asked myself. 'What's the matter with me? I don't have any reason to feel this sad.'

One sunny autumn afternoon my husband and I were sitting on the leather sofa in the study. "We've been married now for three years already," I said to him. "Yes, you're right," he said, "and it's been just as I thought it would be, hasn't it? We have learned to live together, haven't we?" I remained silent and stroked his lifeless hand. Then he kissed me and left. After a few hours I went out as well, crossing the village roads and taking the path that ran alongside the river. I wanted to walk a little beside the water. Leaning on the wooden parapet of the bridge I watched the water run, still and dark, between the grass and the stones, and the sound made me feel a little sleepy. I was getting cold and was about to leave when all of a sudden I spotted my husband scrambling up the grassy ridge of the slope, heading for the woods. I realized that he had seen me as well. He stopped for a moment, uncertain, and then carried on climbing, grasping at the branches of the bushes as he went, until he disappeared in the trees. I returned home and went to the study. I sat on the sofa where just a little while ago he had told me that we had learned to live together. I understood now what he had meant by this. He had learned to lie to me, and it didn't bother him any more. My presence in his house had made him worse, and I too had got worse by living with him. I had become dried up and lifeless. I wasn't suffering, and I didn't feel any pain. I too was lying to him: I was living by his side as if I loved him, when really I didn't love him; I felt nothing for him.

All of a sudden the stairs resounded under his heavy steps. He came into the study, took off his jacket without even looking at me, and put on his old corduroy jacket which he wore around the house. "I want us to leave this place," I said. "I will ask to be moved to another practice, if you want me to," he replied. "But it's you who should want it," I screamed. I realized then that it wasn't true to say that I wasn't suffering; I was suffering unbearably and I was shaking all over. "Once you said to me that I must help you, and that that was why you married me; but why did you marry me?" I sobbed. "Yes, why indeed? What a mistake it has been!" he said, and sat down covering his face with his hands. "I don't want you to go on seeing her. You mustn't see her again," I said bending over him. He pushed me away with an angry gesture, "What do I care about you?" he said. "You're nothing new for me; there's nothing about you which interests me. You're like my mother and my mother's mother, and all the women who have ever lived in this house. You weren't beaten as a child. You didn't have to go hungry. They didn't make you work in the fields from dawn till dusk under the back-breaking sun. Your presence, yes, it gives me peace and quiet, but that's all. I don't know what to do about it, but I can't love you." He took his pipe, filled it meticulously, and lit it, suddenly calm again. "Anyway, all this talk is useless; these things don't matter. Mariuccia is pregnant," he said.

A few days later I went to the coast with the children and the wet nurse. We had planned this trip for a long time, as the children had been ill and they both needed the sea air; my husband was going to accompany us and stay there with us for a month. But, without needing to mention it, it was now understood that he would not come. We stayed by the sea for the whole winter. I wrote to my husband once a week and received a punctual response from him each time. Our letters contained just a few short and rather cold sentences.

We returned at the beginning of spring. My husband was waiting for us at the station. While we travelled through the village in the car I saw Mariuccia pass us with a swollen belly. She walked lightly in spite of the weight of her belly, and the pregnancy had not changed her childish smile. But there was something new in her expression, some sense of submission and shame, and she blushed when she saw me, but not in the same way as she used to blush, with that happy impudence. I thought that soon I would see her carrying a dirty child in her arms, wearing the long clothes which all peasant children have, and that child would be my husband's son, the brother of Luigi and Giorgio. I thought that it would be unbearable to see that child with the long clothes. I wouldn't have been able to continue living with my husband or carry on living in the village. I would leave.

My husband was extremely dispirited. Days and days passed during which he barely uttered a word. He didn't even enjoy being with the children anymore. I saw he had grown old and his clothes had become scruffy; his cheeks were covered in bristly hair. He came home very late at night and sometimes went straight to bed without eating. Sometimes he didn't sleep at all and spent the entire night in the study.

On our return I found the house in complete chaos. Felicetta had grown old; she couldn't remember anything, and argued with the male servant, accusing him of drinking too much. They would exchange violent insults and often I had to intervene to calm them down.

For several days I had a lot to do. The house had to be put in order so that it would be ready for the coming summer. The woollen blankets and cloaks needed to be put away in the cupboards, the armchairs covered in white linen, the curtains taken out on the terrace; the vegetable garden needed sowing, and the roses in the garden needed pruning. I remembered the pride and energy I had given to all these tasks in the early days after we had got married. I had imagined that every simple job was of the highest importance. Since then hardly four years had passed, but how I now saw myself changed! Even physically I looked more like an older woman now. I brushed my hair without a parting, with the bun low down on my neck. Looking at myself in the mirror, I sometimes thought that having my hair combed like that didn't suit me, and it made me look older. But I didn't care about looking pretty anymore. I didn't care about anything.

One evening I was sitting in the dining room with the wet nurse, who was teaching me a knitting stitch. The children were sleeping and my husband had gone to a village a few miles away where somebody had fallen seriously ill. All of a sudden the bell rang and the servant went barefooted to see who it was. I went downstairs as well: it was a boy of about fourteen, and I recognized him as one of Mariuccia's brothers. "They sent me to call the doctor; my sister is not well," he said. "But the doctor isn't here." He shrugged his shoulders and went away. After a while, he came back again. "Hasn't the doctor returned yet?" he asked. "No," I told him, "but I'll let him know." The male servant had already gone to bed, so I told him to get dressed and go and call for the doctor on his bicycle. I went up to my room and started to undress, but I was too anxious and on edge; I felt that I should do something as well. I covered my head with a shawl and went out. I walked through the empty, dark village. In the kitchen Mariuccia's brothers were dozing with their heads resting on the table. The neighbours were huddled by the door talking among themselves. In the room next door Mariuccia was pacing up and down in the small space between the bed and the door; she was crying and walking, leaning against the wall as she went. She went on walking and screaming, and stared at me but didn't seem to recognize who I was. Her mother gave me a resentful and hostile look. I sat on the bed. "The doctor won't be long, will he Signora?" the midwife asked me. "The girl has been in labour for some hours now. She had already lost a lot of blood. The delivery is not going well." "I've sent for him to be called. He should be here soon," I said.

Then Mariuccia fainted and we carried her onto the bed. They needed something from the chemist's and I offered to go myself. When I returned she had come round and had started screaming again. Her cheeks were hot and she struggled around throwing off the covers. She clung to the headboard of the bed and screamed. The midwife came and went with fresh bottles of water. "It's a terrible business," she said in a loud, calm voice. "But we must do something," I said to her. "If my husband is late, we must alert another doctor." "Doctors know lots of clever words, but not much else," her mother said, and she gave me another resentful look, clutching the rosary to her breast. "Women always scream when the baby is about to come," one of the women said.

Mariuccia was writhing on the bed and her hair was all dishevelled. Suddenly, she grabbed hold of me, squeezing me with her dark, bare arms. "Mother of God," she kept saying. The sheets were stained with blood; there was even blood on the ground. The midwife did not leave her side now. "Be strong," she said to her from time to time. Now she was making hoarse sobbing noises. She had bags under her eyes, and her face was dark and covered in sweat: "It's not good, it's not good," the midwife kept repeating. Finally, she received the baby in her hands, lifted it, and shook it. "It's dead," she said, and she threw it down into a corner of the bed. I saw a wrinkled face. It looked like a little Chinese person. The women took it away, bound up in a woollen rag.

Now Mariuccia had stopped screaming; she lay there looking extremely pale, and the blood continued to flow from her body. I saw that there was a little mark of blood on my blouse. "It'll come out with some water," the midwife said to me. "It doesn't matter," I said. "You've helped me a lot tonight," she said. "You're a very courageous lady – truly the wife of a doctor."

One of the neighbours insisted that I should have a little coffee. I followed her into the kitchen and drank a cup of weak, tepid coffee from a glass. When I returned Mariuccia was dead. They told me she had died like that, without having come round from her drowsiness.

They plaited her hair and straightened up the blankets around her. At last my husband arrived. He was holding his leather briefcase; he looked pale and out of breath, and his overcoat was open. I was sitting next to the bed but he did not look at me. He stood in the middle of the room. The mother stood in front of him, tore the briefcase from his hands, and threw it to the ground. "You didn't even come to see her die," she said to him.

I gathered up his briefcase and took my husband's hand. "Let's go," I said to him. He let me lead him across the kitchen, through the murmuring women, and he followed me out. All of a sudden I stopped; it seemed to me right that he should see the little Chinese-looking baby. But where was he? God knows where they had taken him.

As we walked I held him tight, but he did not respond to me in any way, and his arm swung lifelessly by my side. I realized that he was not taking any notice of me and I understood that I mustn't speak, and that I had to be extremely careful with him. He came upstairs with me to the door of our room but then left me and went off to the study, as he had done recently.

It was already nearly light outside; I heard the birds singing in the trees. I went to bed. All of a sudden I realized that I was overcome with a feeling of immense joy. I had no idea that somebody's death could make you so happy, yet I didn't feel guilty for it at all. I had not been happy for some time, and for me this was a completely new feeling, which amazed and transformed me. I also felt full of foolish pride for the way I had conducted myself that night. I knew that my husband could not think of it now, but one day, when he had composed himself a little, he would think of it again, and perhaps he would realize that I had performed well.

All of a sudden a shot rang out through the silence of the house. I got up from my bed screaming and went down the stairs, screaming all the way. I burst into the study and shook his large body which lay motionless on the armchair; his arms were hanging down lifelessly. There was a little blood on the cheeks and lips of that face I knew so well.

Afterwards the house filled up with people. I had to speak and answer every question. The children were taken away. Two days later I accompanied my husband to the cemetery. When I came home I wandered around the rooms in a daze. That house had become dear to me, but I felt as though I didn't have the right to live there, because it didn't belong to me, because I had shared it with a man who had died without uttering a single word to me. Yet, I didn't know where I should go. There wasn't a single place in the world where I wanted to go.

German Soldiers Pass through Erra

ON THE 10TH OF SEPTEMBER a car stopped in the piazza in front of the town hall in Erra. It was a little open-top yellow car which had a long, dusty olive branch hanging from one side. Three men wearing yellow uniforms got out of the vehicle, pulled out a little red book, and began to finger through it.

It was four o'clock in the afternoon. Two days earlier news of the armistice had arrived, out of the blue. At first, nobody had believed it. That same day was market day, and the dusty and treeless main road which ran down into the town (it was the only big road in the village) was filled with people. On both sides of the road and in the piazza there were pigs and hens, baskets of figs, and the ragmen's stalls with their long, pink vests and stockings flapping about. Amid the grunting of the pigs and the sound of the zufoletti,[1] news spread all of a sudden that the war had ended. And it was true – the radio had said so. Since that moment people had not stopped hugging one another, and everybody went to the local bar and sang all night long. The shoemaker in Borgo San Giacomo, Spondò, seemed drunk with joy – he was a communist and as a young man had often been beaten up because of it; he'd even been forced to spend time in exile on the islands. Now he charged up and down the village on his bicycle, stopping every passer-by to tell them, 'Spondò has won the war.'

On the 9th, nobody had had the faintest idea what was happening. In Erra, the electricity had been cut off and the radio had fallen silent. On the 10th, the yellow vehicle with three uniformed men arrived. It was the same piazza where the villagers had held market and the people had sung and danced at the news of the armistice. It was the same piazza where, on the evening of the 26th of July, they had carried all the Fascist files and pissed on them by way of insult.

When the men in yellow uniforms arrived news immediately spread through the village that they were foreign soldiers, who spoke among themselves in a language which nobody understood. Some people thought that they were English and straightaway went out to see. But Secondina said: "They're Germans!" Secondina was Bissecolo's wife. Bissecolo had lived in Germany for five years as a child, and decided to speak to the newly arrived soldiers in German. But Secondina said, "Run for your life, they're Germans!"

---

1 Small, flute-like instruments traditionally crafted from forest wood in Italy. Akin to the English flageolet, the *zufolo* produces a high-pitched, whistle-like sound.

So everyone ran away. They didn't know where to go, so they ran down the little path which went into the fields; the women held the children in their arms and were in floods of tears. "What will they do to us now?" they said. "Will they kill us and our children straightaway?" Those who had children at the nun's convent school waited close by the convent's bell, each one anxious to collect their children and take them down the path which led to the fields. After a while, the town was totally empty and silent, except for the occasional sound of the convent bell ringing out.

The men in uniform didn't seem surprised. They said nothing. Only Bissecolo – the one who spoke German – stayed in the piazza; he wasn't afraid of the Germans. He stood in front of them in his green corduroy suit and told them how he had spent five years in Germany as a young man. All of a sudden, the men asked him where the local carabinieri[2] sergeant was.

But the carabinieri sergeant had already been alerted and had left the barracks in order to meet the soldiers in the piazza. He was a tall young man, with an olive complexion, slick dark hair, and slightly crooked legs. One of the soldiers moved forward to speak to him while the others remained with Bissecolo in front of the car.

The soldier asked him: "How do you get to Ascoli Piceno?" He was a young man with a rosy complexion and curly chestnut-coloured hair. His large and powerful thighs stood out against the light material of his trousers. Around his waist he wore a large leather belt which had a pistol tucked into it. The carabinieri sergeant looked green in the face. He could feel sweat breaking on his forehead but did not dare to wipe it away.

"We want to go to Ascoli Piceno," the soldier said. "Can you tell us if this is the right road?" He had a calm voice which was persuasive and kind. The carabinieri sergeant swallowed hard. Finally he dug out a handkerchief (which had a black border since his mother had recently died) and very slowly mopped his brow and under his chin, wiping his hands as well.

The soldier said, "They told us that you can get there by going through this way too. Don't you have a map?" He spoke Italian very well. He had green eyes and dark eyelashes which were very long

---

2   The *carabinieri* are the official military police in Italy, their full title being *Arma dei Carabinieri* ('Force of Carabinieri'). They operate both as a military and police corps, with companies or stations based in most Italian towns.

and thick. His breath smelt of wine. The carabinieri sergeant said, "Come with me to the station."

After half an hour, the soldiers got back in their car, which roared off towards Montereale. They had taken the carabinieri sergeant's map with them. Bissecolo had given them two bottles of beer. He said afterwards that they had threatened him with a pistol, but this was certainly not true; he was a notorious liar.

Once the soldiers had gone the people came back from the fields, the women returned carrying their children in arms, and everybody filled the piazza and Secondina's shop to debate what had happened. Bissecolo had gone to the town with his handcart; everybody said that he had gone in order to avoid being beaten up because he had spoken in German and made a gift of the bottles. Secondina wasn't to blame for the husband she had; it was obvious from her tubercular face that she had been the first one to suffer by him – her husband offering gifts of beer to the enemy while at the same time denying her even bread to eat. They all asked her what those three soldiers had said to Bissecolo, and she told them that they had said they were retreating to Northern Italy for fear of the Americans. Nobody believed that they had said this, but Secondina swore blind that this was exactly what they had said. Giuliano della Torretta said that they should have taken them as prisoners, but instead that idiot of a carabinieri sergeant had let them get away and had even given them a map so that they might find their way more easily.

The following morning a new German vehicle came by, but this time it was a lorry carrying six or seven men holding rifles. The priest's brother, Giuliano della Torretta, and Loretuccio the baker were in the piazza. It speeded past, raising a great cloud of dust, and when it had disappeared behind the bend they looked at each other like fools, and Loretuccio took off his cap and threw it to the ground. Giuliano della Torretta said, "We shouldn't have let them pass! What idiots we've been!" They went to fetch a beam from Loretuccio's house and placed it across the road to act as a barrier.

After a little while another lorry came by and pulled to one side in front of the beam. There were five Germans on board. Loretuccio and Giuliano della Torretta were leaning against the wall, but the priest's brother left with the excuse that he was suffering from stomach pains. The Germans shouted something in their own language, but Loretuccio and Giuliano della Torretta stood motionless, smoking and looking down at the ground. Then one of the soldiers drew his pistol, hastily repeating what he had just said, his neck swelling up as he spoke. Loretuccio and Giuliano della Torretta lifted the beam out of the way, and the lorry disappeared behind the bend.

Loretuccio and Giuliano della Torretta returned home. Giuliano della Torretta lived alone, but Loretuccio had seven children – like the seven deadly sins – and there was never enough food to go round. Even though it was only thanks to a miracle and the good grace of Our Lady that he still was alive, the face of that soldier with the pistol remained firmly fixed in his mind.

From that moment on large numbers of cars began passing through, raising great clouds of dust as they disappeared round the bend in the road. Some of them carried an olive branch and the Red Cross flag on the roof; some were long and shiny like fish; some were tiny and streaked with green, and they sped away as quick as lightning. Erra had never seen so much activity; Attilio's dog Boschetto was run over, and he cried about it for a whole day. Some vehicles were Italian and had Genova or Torino written on the back, but were in fact filled with German soldiers who were dressed in uniform and carried their rifles levelled. People no longer ran away to the fields, but instead looked on in disbelief from their doorsteps.

On the 15th of September, news came that the Germans were occupying the neighbouring town. They had requisitioned two hotels and the petrol reserves. They were strutting about the beautiful town as if it was their own, sitting around eating ice cream and drinking wine.

The carabinieri sergeant had discarded his uniform and no longer seemed to be the same man; his two colleagues also stopped wearing their uniforms and carrying their rifles. Arielle, the younger carabiniere, had a large patch on his trousers and no longer frightened anybody; the girls stopped paying him any attention and he became very depressed as a result. One day, the Republican Fascists came as well, but they didn't frighten anybody as everybody knew who they were: one was Vargas, who had once been the mayor in Erra; the other was the son of the chemist in Montereale. They went to the vet, took away his boots, and smashed his radio to pieces simply because he had been listening to the news from London. There were no other radios in Erra, and so nobody knew anything about the war anymore, or anything else.

On the 5th of October, two English prisoners appeared in Erra. One was a black man. They came down from the mountain; their shirts were ripped but they had smart, solid shoes which you could tell had come from London. As soon as they arrived in the piazza everybody ran to welcome them as if they were liberators. Loretuccio was anxious to ask them when their comrades were coming, and everybody felt happier now that these two prisoners were in the village. Nonetheless German cars continued to shoot through the town like arrows, disappearing far away round the bend in the road; each one that passed was like a sharp pain in the stomach, and the sound of the car horns lacerated the air.

They took these prisoners to the carabinieri sergeant, who swallowed hard and sent for Giuliano della Torretta. Wearing a cap pulled right down over his eyes and clenching a pipe between his teeth, Giuliano della Torretta arrived and the carabinieri sergeant asked him where on earth they were going to hide them. Giuliano della Torretta thought for a moment and then remembered Nazarena, who lived some distance away from the village, on the banks of the river. So he and the carabinieri sergeant took the prisoners there. Nazarena was an old spinster. She was blind in one eye and had scars on her face because she had fallen into a fire as a child. Nazarena wanted the white prisoner, but not the black one. It took a while to convince her to take them both.

On the 7th of October, two days after the prisoners had arrived, a German soldier came to Cagnaccetta's bar. He was a sergeant and said his name was Otto Keller. He spoke a little Italian, and before he had even sat down he spoke about how he had nobody left because his entire family had died during a bombing raid in Cologne. He hugged Cagnaccetta and called her 'Mutti.' It was clear before he even touched a drink that he wasn't sober – he'd obviously had something to drink before arriving. Cagnaccetta pushed her fourteen-year-old daughter away into the lavatory and locked the door shut because she was frightened he might turn nasty. The soldier was young and chubby with a pale, round, moon-like face. He embraced Cagnaccetta and danced her round in a circle, drunk as he was. Cagnaccetta had a grey and white handkerchief tied in her hair. She was terrified but pretended to laugh nonetheless, slapping the German on the back, though never taking her eyes off the lavatory door. The bar was empty that evening until all of a sudden Antonino della Trabanda arrived; it was the devil himself who brought him there. He went in and saw the German dancing round the table with Cagnaccetta and singing in his own language. When Cagnaccetta saw Antonino she gave him a quick look as if to say, 'Go! Get away.' Antonino quickly went back down the steps in order to fetch the hunting rifle he had buried in the vegetable garden just in case one day he needed it. He had wanted to kill a German for a long time, and he thought about it all the time with a mania which bordered on obsession. He returned with his rifle and fired straight at the soldier, who collapsed to the ground, smashing the bottle of wine as he fell. Cagnaccetta started screaming, and the girl in the lavatory started screaming as well, banging on the door with her fists. The carabinieri sergeant arrived with Bissecolo, the priest's brother, and Loretuccio, and they all stood and looked at the soldier and didn't know what to do. Cagnaccetta was screaming as if possessed by the devil, and Antonino Trabanda stood motionless, still holding his rifle levelled. All of a sudden he began shaking and the rifle fell from his hands.

Three hours later a shiny grey police car arrived along with two motorcyclists who were carrying sub-machine guns. Everybody fled from the village into the fields, but Giuliano della Torretta did not move; he was someone who didn't like to run away, and he was not afraid of dying. So it was that he stayed there to wait for death on the doorstep of his own home, his cap pulled down over his eyes and his pipe clenched between his teeth. But when the German officer came and seized him by the jacket, he pulled out a pistol and started firing. By bad luck he missed everybody, and they killed him where he stood.

They found Antonino della Trabanda in the priest's vineyard – he had not had time to get any further away, shaken up as he was by what he had done. They found the carabinieri sergeant on the road to Borgo San Giacomo together with his sister, who had run away carrying the quilt from her bed with her. So they caught her too and took them back to the piazza.

In the piazza, they killed them one after another, Antonino Trabanda and Spondò, the carabinieri sergeant and his sister, Loretuccio and the priest's brother; they also killed Bissecolo by mistake, he who spoke German so well. The others in the fields heard the sound of the shots and, with their faces pressed into the grass, shuddered, full of a desire never to return home again.

The Mother

THEIR MOTHER WAS SMALL AND THIN with slightly hunched shoulders; she always wore a blue skirt and a red woollen blouse. Her curly hair was short and dark and she would grease it with oil to try to make it lie flat; every day she plucked her eyebrows, turning them into two little dark fish darting towards her temples, and put yellow powder on her face. She was very young. They didn't know how old she was but she looked much younger than the mothers of their school friends; the boys always stared in amazement when they saw their friends' mothers, who were all so fat and old. She smoked a lot and her fingers were stained by smoke; in the evening she even smoked in bed before going to sleep. The three of them all slept together in the large double bed with the yellow quilt, their mother on the side nearest the door; on the bedside table there was a lamp with the shade wrapped up in a red rag because she liked to read and smoke in the evening. Sometimes she came home very late, and the boys would wake up and ask her where she had been: she usually answered, 'to the cinema' or 'at a girlfriend's house' – they did not know who this friend could be as no friend had ever come to the house to see their mother. She would tell them to turn their backs while she got undressed, and they would hear the quick rustle of her clothes, see the shadows dancing on the walls, and then she would slip into the bed next to them, a thin body in a cold silk blouse. They kept their distance because she always complained that they would crowd her and kick her during the night: sometimes she would turn the light off to make them go to sleep while she smoked in the dark.

Their mother was not an important person. The important people were their grandmother, their grandfather, and Aunt Clementina, who lived in the country and came to visit every now and then, bringing chestnuts and maize flour; Diomira the maid was important, and so was the frail porter Giovanni, who made cane chairs. They were all very important to the two boys because they were strong people who could be trusted, who knew the difference between right and wrong, who were very good at everything they did, and were always full of common sense and strength; they were the sort of people who could protect you from storms and thieves. When the boys were left alone in the house with their mother they felt scared just as if they were all alone; how could they know the difference between right and wrong when their mother never said what was right and wrong? At the most she would complain in a weary voice, 'Stop making so much noise, I've got a headache.' If they asked whether they were allowed to do something, she would say at once, 'ask your Grandma,' or she would first say 'yes,' then 'no' and it ended up being a muddle. When they went out alone with their mother they felt uncertain and uneasy because she always got lost and had to ask a policeman for directions, and she had such a timid and silly manner when she was in shops asking for things to buy. She would always leave something behind in the shop – her gloves, her bag, or her scarf – and they would have to go back to retrieve them and the boys would feel ashamed.

The clothes she kept in her drawers were all of a muddle, and she left everything strewn around, and Diomira would grumble about her when she tidied the room in the morning. She would even call their grandmother to come and see, and together they would collect up the stockings and clothes and throw away the cigarette ash that was scattered all over the place. In the morning, their mother would go shopping: when she returned home she would bang the shopping bag on the marble table in the kitchen, get on her bicycle, and rush off to the office where she worked. Diomira would look at the contents of the shopping bag, feel the meat and every orange one by one, grumble, and call their grandmother to see how awful the meat was. Their mother would return home at two o'clock when everyone had already eaten and would eat in a rush with a newspaper propped against her glass and then slip away again on her bicycle to work; they saw her again for a moment at dinner, but after eating she would almost always slip away somewhere else.

The boys did their homework in the bedroom. At the head of the bed was a large portrait of their father, with his square dark beard, bald head, and tortoise-shell rimmed glasses; on the table there was another smaller portrait of him holding the youngest of the boys. Their father had died when they were very small and they could not remember anything about him. However the oldest boy could dimly recall an afternoon long gone spent at Aunt Clementina's house in the country: their father was pushing him on the grass in a green wheelbarrow; he had since found some parts of that wheelbarrow, a handle and the wheel in Aunt Clémentina's loft; when it was new it had been a beautiful wheelbarrow and he had been proud to own it; his father ran while he pushed him, and his long beard waved about. They did not know anything about their father, but they thought he must have been one of those people who were strong and knew the difference between right and wrong; when their grandfather or Diomira got angry with their mother their grandmother would say that they must have pity on their mother as she had been very unlucky and that if Eugenio, the boys' father, were still alive she would have been a different person, but that she had had the misfortune to lose her husband when she was still very young. For a short time there had also been a paternal grandmother whom they never saw because she lived in France, but who wrote and sent little presents at Christmas, but eventually she died as she was very old.

For their afternoon snack they ate chestnuts, or bread with olive oil and vinegar, and if they had finished their homework they were allowed to go down to the small piazza to play among the ruins of the public baths which had been blown up during a bombing. In the small piazza there were lots of pigeons and they would take them bread, or they made Diomira give them a packet of old rice. There they also met up with all the local children, school friends and others whom they would also see at the parish hall on Sundays, when they played football with Don Vigliani, who would pull up his black cassock to get at the ball. Sometimes they used to play football in the small piazza as well, or cops and robbers. Every now and then their grandmother would come to the balcony and shout down, telling them not to hurt themselves. Looking up from the gloomy piazza, it was nice to see the windows lit up in the flat on the third floor, and to know that they could go back there to warm up by the stove and take refuge from the night. Their grandmother would sit in the kitchen with Diomira mending sheets; their grandfather stayed in the dining room wearing his hat and smoking a pipe. Their grandmother was very fat and dressed in black. On her breast, she wore a large locket which contained a portrait of their Uncle Oreste, who had died in the war; she was very good at cooking pizzas and many other things. Sometimes their grandmother would hold them on her knees, even now when they were quite big; she was fat and had a large floppy bosom; you could see underneath the neckline of her dress a big white woollen vest with a coloured border which she had knitted herself. She would take them on her knees and whisper sweet and tender words to them, speaking in dialect. Then she would pull out a long iron pin from her hair bun and would clean their ears, and they would squeal and try to run away, and then their grandfather with his pipe would come to the door.

Their grandfather had once been a Greek and Latin high-school teacher. Now he was retired and was writing a Greek grammar book; many of his old students would come to see him now and then, and Diomira would have to make coffee; in the lavatory there were sheets from exercise books with translations from Greek and Latin and his corrections on them in red and blue ink. Their grandfather had a little white beard, a bit like a goat, and they were not allowed to be noisy because he had fragile nerves from the many years that he had spent teaching. He was always a bit anxious because prices kept going up and their grandmother had to nag him in the mornings as he always seemed amazed at the amount of money she wanted; he said that maybe Diomira was stealing their sugar and secretly making herself cups of coffee, and Diomira would hear this and run over and shout at him that the coffee was for the students who were forever coming round. But these were little incidents which quickly fizzled out, and the boys weren't frightened as they were when there was an argument between the grandfather and their mother. This happened on those occasions when their mother returned home late at night; he would come out of his room in bare feet wearing his overcoat on top of his pyjamas, and they would both shout at each other. He would say, 'I know where you've been, I know where you've been, I know what you are,' and their mother would reply, 'What do I care? Now look, you've woken up the children,' and he would say, 'What do you care about the children? Don't speak because I know what you are. You're a bitch. You run around at night like the mad bitch you are.' Then their grandmother and Diomira would come out in their nightshirts and drag him back to his room, hushing him as they went. Their mother would slip into bed and weep under the sheets, her grating sobs resounding across the dark room; the boys were sure their grandfather was right – their mother was wrong to go to the cinema and visit her friends at night. They felt very frightened and unhappy, and would stay huddled up in the large, soft, warm bed, and the biggest boy, who was in the middle, would push himself to one side so as not to touch his mother's body; he felt there was something disgusting about his mother crying into the wet pillow – 'a boy feels disgusted with his mother when she cries,' he thought. They did not speak of these arguments between their mother and grandfather, carefully avoiding speaking about them. But they both felt for each other deeply and huddled together tight during the night when their mother cried; in the morning they felt a little ashamed of each other because they had been hugging so tightly as if to protect each other and because there was something they didn't want to talk about. Yet they quickly forgot about having been unhappy; the new day began and they would go to school, and on the way they would meet up with their friends and play for a little outside the school before going in.

In the grey light of the morning, their mother would get up; with her petticoat pulled up around her waist, she would wash her neck and arms standing bent over the little washbasin. She always tried to hide her scrawny dark shoulders and small naked breasts from them but they would catch sight of her in the mirror; in the cold her nipples were dark and erect; she would lift her arms and powder her armpits, which were covered in curly thick hair. When she had finished dressing she would begin to pluck her eyebrows, standing close to the mirror and pursing her lips tightly; then she would rub cream into her face, shake the bright pink powder puff vigorously, and powder herself: at that point her face turned all yellow. Sometimes she was quite cheerful in the mornings and wanted to speak with the children. She would ask about school and their friends and she would tell them something about when she had been at school; she had had a teacher called 'Signorina Dirce' and she was an old spinster who wanted people to think she was young. Then she would put on her coat, fetch the shopping bag, bend down to kiss the boys, and run off with her scarf wrapped around her head, her face all perfumed and covered in yellow powder.

The boys found it strange to think that they had come from her. It would have been much less strange to have been born of their grandmother or Diomira and their large warm bodies which protected you from being scared, and from storms and thieves. It was very strange to think that she was their mother, the one who had once held them in her tiny stomach. Since they had learned that children stay in their mother's stomach before being born they had felt very surprised and also a little ashamed that *that* stomach had held them once upon a time. She had also given them milk from her breasts; this seemed something even more incredible. But now she no longer had small children to breastfeed and rock, and every day they saw her slip off on her bicycle after shopping, happy and carefree. Surely she did not belong to them; they couldn't count on her. They couldn't ask her anything: there were other mothers, their friends' mothers, whom you could clearly ask all manner of things; their friends would run to their mothers once school was finished and ask all kinds of things; they made them blow their noses and button up their coats, and showed them homework and comics. These mothers were quite old, wore hats or veils or fur collars, and almost every day would come to speak to the teacher; they were people like their grandmother or Diomira: large, gentle, and imperious people who did not make mistakes, people who did not lose things, who did not leave their drawers in a muddle, who did not come home late at night. But their mother would slip away after shopping; if truth be told she didn't know how to shop properly; she would get mixed up at the butcher's and often they would also short-change her. She would slip away and it would be impossible to reach her wherever it was she went. Deep down they admired her greatly when she slipped away; they wondered what her office would be like as she did not speak of it often. She probably had to type and write letters in French and English; who knows, perhaps she was quite good at this.

One day they had gone to take a walk with Don Vigliani with the other boys from the youth club, when coming home they saw their mother in a café in the suburbs. She was sitting inside – they could see her through the windows – and a man was sitting with her. Their mother had put on her tartan scarf, and her old crocodile skin bag – which they knew so well – was on the table. The man had a large light overcoat and a chestnut-coloured moustache and he was smiling as he spoke to her; their mother looked happy and relaxed, as she never looked when she was at home. She was looking at the man and they were holding hands, and she did not see the boys: the boys continued to walk next to Don Vigliani, who told everyone to hurry up as they needed to catch the tram. When they were on the tram the smallest child went up to his brother and said, "Did you see mamma?" His brother answered, "No, I didn't see her." The little boy laughed quietly and said: "Of course you saw her, it was definitely mamma and there was a man with her." The older boy turned his head away; he was big, nearly thirteen years old: his little brother annoyed him because he made him feel sorry for him. He didn't know why, but he made him feel sorry for him; he even felt sorry for himself and did not want to think of what he had seen – he wanted to pretend that he had seen nothing.

They said nothing to their grandmother. In the morning while their mother was getting dressed, the little boy said: "Yesterday when we went for a walk with Don Vigliani, we saw you and there was a man with you." Their mother turned around with a jolt and looked at him angrily: the little black fish on her forehead quivered and joined up together. She said, "It wasn't me, what nonsense; you know I have to stay at the office until late in the evening. You must have got it wrong." At that point the elder boy interrupted with a tired and calm voice, "No, it wasn't you. It was just somebody that looked like you." Both boys understood that they must forget about that memory, and they both tried as hard as they could to get rid of it.

But one day the man with the light overcoat came to their house. He wasn't wearing the overcoat because it was summer; he had blue glasses and a light cotton suit, and he asked permission to take off his jacket while they ate. Their grandfather and their grandmother had gone to Milan to meet with some relatives and Diomira had gone to her village, so they were alone with their mother. So the man came and there was quite a nice lunch. Their mother had brought nearly everything at the rosticceria:[1] there was chicken with fried potatoes which came from the shop, and their mother had made pasta which was good – the sauce was only a little bit burned. There was also some wine. Their mother was nervous and cheerful; she wanted to say lots of things at the same time; she wanted to talk to the man about the boys and to the boys about the man. The man was called Max and had been in Africa; he had lots of pictures of Africa which he showed to them. There was a picture of one of his monkeys, and the boys asked him a lot about this monkey – it was so intelligent and he loved it and it had such a silly and cute manner when it wanted a sweet. But he had left it in Africa because it was ill and he was scared it would die on the steamship. The boys became friends with this Max. He promised to take them to the cinema one time. They showed him their books although they didn't have many; he asked if they had read *Saturnino Farandola* and they said no, and he said that he would give it to them as a present, and also *Robinson delle Praterie* as it was very good. After lunch, their mother told them to go and play in the parish hall. They would have preferred to stay with Max. They complained a little but both their mother and Max told them they must go; and in the evening when they returned to the house Max was gone. Their mother prepared dinner in a hurry, caffelatte and a potato salad. They were happy and wanted to talk about Africa and the monkey; indeed they were extraordinarily happy and they didn't know why; and their mother too seemed happy and chatted about things, about a monkey that she had once seen dancing on a hurdy-gurdy. Then she told them to go to bed and said she had to pop out for a moment, and that they shouldn't be worried as there was no need to be; she bent down to kiss them and told them that there was no point in telling their grandmother and grandfather about Max as they did not like receiving guests.

---

1 A *rosticceria* is a shop in Italy which specializes in selling roast meat and other prepared food.

So they remained alone with their mother for a few days. They ate unusual things because their mother didn't want to cook: ham and jam and caffelatte and fried things from the rosticceria. Then they washed their plates together. But when their grandfather and grandmother returned home they were relieved; once again the tablecloth appeared along with the glasses and everything else that you need at lunchtime. Their grandmother – with her soft body and familiar smell – sat as she always did in the rocking chair; their grandmother could not run away – she was too old and too fat – and it was nice to have somebody at home who could never run away.

The boys never said anything about Max to their grandmother. They waited for the *Saturnino Farandola* book and they waited for Max to take them to the cinema and show them more pictures of the monkey. Once or twice they asked their mother when they would go to the cinema with Signor Max. But their mother told them brusquely that Signor Max had gone now. The youngest boy asked if maybe Max had gone to Africa. Their mother did not reply at all. But he thought that he must certainly have gone to Africa to get his monkey back. He imagined that one day or another he would come to collect them at school, with a black servant and the monkey hanging around his neck. They started school again and their Aunt Clementina came to stay with them for a little while; she brought a bag of pears and apples which she cooked in the oven with marsala and sugar. Their mother was in a very bad mood and argued continuously with their grandfather. She came home late at night and lay awake smoking. She had lost a lot of weight and had practically stopped eating. Her face became increasingly smaller and more yellow; now she also wore black eyeshadow. She would spit inside a little box and with a little brush pull the black over where she had spat. She put on a lot of powder, and when their grandmother tried to take some of it off with a handkerchief, she would pull her head out of the way. She hardly ever spoke, and when she did it seemed an enormous effort, her voice becoming feeble. One day she came home at about six o'clock; it was strange – usually she came home later. Then she locked herself in the bedroom. The youngest boy came to knock as he needed an exercise book, but their mother replied from inside in an angry voice that she wanted to sleep and that they should leave her alone. The boy explained timidly that he needed the exercise book, and so she came to open the door and her face was all swollen and wet. The boy understood that she was crying and turned to his grandmother and said: "Mamma is crying." Their grandmother and Aunt Clementina spoke quietly between themselves; they were talking about their mother but it wasn't clear what they were saying.

One night their mother did not return home. Their grandfather came to look for her many times, barefoot, with his coat over his pyjamas; their grandmother came too and the boys slept badly; they could hear their grandfather and grandmother walking around the house, opening and closing the windows. The boys were very frightened. Then in the morning they telephoned from the police station; their mother had been found dead in a hotel; she had taken poison, and had left a letter. Their grandfather and Aunt Clementina went, their grandmother screamed, and the boys were sent to an old lady on the floor below, who kept repeating, "Heartless, leaving two little souls like that." They brought their mother home. The boys went to see her when they had laid her on the bed; Diomira had dressed her in her patent shoes and the red silk dress that she had worn when she got married – she looked small, like a small dead doll.

It was strange to see flowers and candles in their room. Diomira, Aunt Clementina, and their grandmother were kneeling down in prayer. They said that she had taken the poison by mistake; the priest would not come to bless her if he knew that in fact the opposite was true. Diomira said to the boys that they must kiss her; they felt terribly ashamed and one by one kissed her cold cheek. Then there was the funeral, which lasted a long time. They crossed the whole city and felt very tired – Don Vigliani was also there, as were lots of children from school and from the parish hall. The weather was cold, and a strong wind blew at the cemetery. When they returned home, their grandmother started to cry and wail in front of the bicycle in the hall; it seemed as if the slight figure with the scarf flapping in the wind was about to slip away again. Don Vigliani said that now she was in Paradise, maybe because he didn't know that she had done it on purpose, or because he did know but pretended not to. The boys did not know if Paradise really existed, because their grandfather said it didn't, and the grandmother said it did, and their mother had once told them that Paradise with little angels and beautiful music didn't exist. Rather, the dead went to a place that was neither good nor bad, where you didn't want anything, and because you don't want anything you rest and find peace.

The boys went to Aunt Clementina's house in the country for some time. Everybody was very good to them, and kissed and cuddled them, and they felt very ashamed. They never spoke about their mother between themselves, or even of Signor Max; in Aunt Clementina's loft they found a copy of *Saturnino Farandola* and they read it and thought it was very good. But the elder boy thought often about their mother, how he had seen her that day sitting in the café with Max holding her hands and with her relaxed and happy expression; it made him think that maybe their mother had taken poison because Max had gone back to Africa forever. The boys played with Aunt Clementina's dog, a lovely dog called Bubi, and learned how to climb trees, as before they didn't know how. They also went swimming in the river, and it was nice to go home to Aunt Clementina's in the evening and do crosswords all together. The boys were very happy living with their Aunt Clementina. Then they went back home to their grandmother and they were very happy. Their grandmother sat in her rocking chair, and wanted to clean their ears with her hairpins. On Sundays they would go to the cemetery – Diomira would go with them as well – and they bought flowers; on their way home they would stop in a bar to have a drink of hot punch. When they were at the cemetery, in front of the tomb, their grandmother prayed and cried, but it was very hard to believe that the tombs, the crosses, and the cemetery had anything to do with their mother, who would be short-changed at the butcher's and slip away on her bicycle, and smoke, and lose her way, and sob at night. The bed was now very big for them, and they had one pillow each. They did not think of their mother very often because it hurt a little and made them feel ashamed. If they tried at times to think of her, each would do so in silence, on his own: and it gradually became increasingly difficult to piece together an image of her short curly hair, the little fishes on her forehead and her lips. She wore a lot of yellow face powder, this they remembered well. Little by little, she became just a yellow dot on which it was impossible to distinguish the outline of her face and cheeks. However, they now realized that they had not loved her very much. Maybe she had not loved them much either, for if she had loved them she wouldn't have taken poison – that was what they had heard from Diomira, the porter, the lady on the floor below, and many others. The years passed and the boys grew up and many things happened and that face that they had never loved very much eventually vanished forever.

The Marshal

THAT DAY THEY HAD GUESTS, and everybody ate ice cream from pretty little plates which were shaped like strawberry leaves. Uncle Giovanni told a long story which lasted right through lunch, but the children had not bothered to listen.

"And that's why they told me to have a word with the marshal," he said at the end.

It must have been a funny story because everyone was laughing; their grandmother was almost choking, throwing herself back in her armchair. The children asked if they could take some fruit and go outside, and she indicated they could, without listening to them and continuing to cough and laugh. Each of the children took a handful of cherries and ran away. As they ran across the garden they were joined by Memi, the thin, shaven-headed son of the caretaker, and everyone went to 'the usual place.' That place was the cellar; you got there from the garden by climbing through a window. Inside there was an old sofa with broken springs, and the gardener's tools in a corner.

Silvio jumped eagerly onto the sofa and began to leap about wildly shouting: "The marshal!" because he loved the word so much. His sister Nennella, who copied everything he did, also began jumping and shouting, and after a while all four children were dancing on the sofa repeating one after another, "marshal, marshal!" "Come out marshal!" screamed Paolo, now exhausted, letting himself fall down onto his stomach. And then an extraordinary thing happened. A marshal climbed through the window and sat down on a trunk in the corner of the cellar.

He was tall, thin, and hunched, with a bald red head and long blondish white side-whiskers. What was really splendid about him was his uniform, which was a beautiful vibrant blue colour, with two rows of shiny buttons.

"Next time I come I shall bring my stuffed bear with me," he said as he wiped the sweat from his head with a handkerchief. "I would have brought him today, but I wasn't sure if you would have welcomed him properly. He might have scared you as well."

"But how can a stuffed bear scare anybody?" asked Silvio, who was the least timid of them all.

"Well how do you know a stuffed bear isn't as good as the real thing?" said the marshal. "I give you my word of honour that my friend is a beast of the very finest stock. His fur is really extraordinary ... just like silk," he added as an aside.

"Like silk," echoed the children with their eyes wide open. "Is it black or white?"

"Black!" said the marshal, looking shocked. "Blacker than black. So black that at night you can't see him, except for his shimmering eyes."

"I thought only cats had luminous eyes," said Nennella, a girl who studied a lot at school.

"Bears do too," the marshal declared, "yes, bears do too. But enough of that ... Haven't you got any more interesting subjects to talk about?"

"Subjects?" murmured the frightened children. "No."

"Oh well, never mind. What's that you have there? Cherries? I like cherries. Why haven't you offered me any? How rude you children are." All of a sudden, he shoved an entire bunch of cherries in his mouth and swallowed them.

"Awful," he said spluttering, "a real load of rubbish. The trees in my little fruit garden would be ashamed if they produced cherries like those – *they* are exemplary trees. I planted them all myself, one after the other; I've watched them grow up and they're like children to me. When I come home they rustle gently, as if they're saying hello. I pass, and they rustle, they rustle gently. But they don't care the least bit for my maid. She's quite a surly woman, but not nasty. She certainly wouldn't be happy to know that I'm here."

"Why?" asked the children.

"It's the way she is – she can't stand children. It's just her character. She's always grumbling, but she's fond of me, and she knows how to cook lovely soups. Some of her soups ... Mmmm!" The marshal made his tongue click. "She is also very good at washing my ship. Every morning she cleans and washes it."

"You have a ship?" asked Silvio, showing great interest.

"Yes, a ship! Why shouldn't I have a ship?" said the marshal with indignation. "Of course I've got one. And it's the most beautiful ship that has ever been seen. A stupendous ship."

"Does it go on the sea?"

The marshal heaved a long sigh, and his face became rather sad.

"How beautiful it used to be," he said. "I used to go to sea with my ship and all my men whom I commanded. There wasn't another ship in the sea that went as fast as ours, and when we put the sails up it seemed like we were flying."

"But what about the men? Where are they now?"

"They're dead," said the marshal with a sob in his voice. "All dead. Eaten by fish. Ah, what men they were! That was the life! My enemies ruined me. They took everything from me. Everything was destroyed; the men are dead and the ship has become useless – I keep it in the pond down from my house."

He was silent and his head was a little lowered; the children noticed that he was crying. It was sad to see the marshal cry. The children surrounded him in silence not knowing what to do.

"But it doesn't matter, I'll have my revenge," said the marshal all of a sudden. "I'll take my revenge on those people who did me harm. Will you help me? You'll help me, won't you?"

"We'll help you! We'll help you! We'll get revenge! Revenge, revenge!" sang the children in chorus as they jumped around enthusiastically on the sofa.

The marshal came back often – he even got into the habit of coming every day, and this filled all the children with joy. They were full of admiration and affection for him. They marvelled at the sight of his buttons and beautiful long side-whiskers, and they willingly gave him their snacks, which he would devour in a flash. Then he would say, 'Disgusting, a load of rubbish.' But even this made the children happy. The adults didn't like them spending all their time in the dusty cellar while the sun was shining outside, and they used to say: 'Goodness only knows what they get up to down there.' Nevertheless, as soon as they were free they would hurry down to the cellar, and the marshal would not be late in arriving. What a wonderful time they all spent there together. He would sit down, wipe the sweat from his brow, and say: 'It's a pity, I haven't brought my bear.'

"Yes, why haven't you brought him?" Memi asked in an insolent way which made him appear quite unpleasant.

"My poor friend was very disappointed that he couldn't come," sighed the marshal. "He gets very bored all alone without me. But what can you do? Such a long journey could make him tired."

"Has he ever been ill?" the children asked.

"Oh yes, my dear old thing does get ill sometimes," said the marshal. "I even have to give him medicine. He fixes his eyes on me as if to beg me not to, but I have to give him the medicine anyway to help him get better."

"What does he eat?"

"All kinds of things, all kinds of things. I go hunting in the woods and I bring him a hare, a thrush or something. I bring it and he eats it."

"But he's stuffed!" protested Memi.

The marshal looked at him pitiably.

"Children like you ought to have their tongues cut out," he said.

"One morning you'll get up and you'll want to ask for a caffelatte, but you won't be able to, because you'll have had your tongue cut out."

"My father goes hunting sometimes," said Paolo. "Do you like hunting as well?"

"It's my favourite hobby. I go into the woods. You should see the wood I own, you couldn't imagine a bigger one, and the trees are very tall and green, much taller and greener than the trees here. They're real trees!"

"Are there any strawberries there?"

"There are lots of strawberries in my wood," said the marshal. "How could you think that there wouldn't be any strawberries? They are exquisite strawberries, beautifully sweet. You can taste them if you go down there."

"You must take us one time," said the children.

"Oh yes, no doubt, but you know I can't bear impatient children. No question, you'll come. Just simply go to sleep and you'll get there. Or you can get there another way."

"How?"

"By flying," said the marshal mysteriously. "If you hold onto the tails of my overcoat you can fly."

"It must be amazing! Let's go soon, now!" shouted the children.

"But it's dangerous," said the marshal with a stern expression, "very dangerous. A hurricane could surprise us. What would happen then? You get thrown all over the place; your head spins, and you don't even know where you are. Then you hear a frightening rumble. Then sometimes you swallow a cloud. Some clouds have a nice taste, but others are horribly salty."

"Maybe those are the ones which come from the sea," said Nennella.

"Exactly. But then it's so beautiful when you get there. You can't imagine how beautiful it is. It's not like here. For a start, you can smell the stench here."

"But the rest of the house doesn't smell like this cellar," the children were quick to answer.

"Maybe it's not all like this, but more or less," said the marshal affirmatively. "In any case, it's a thousand times better down there. You must come. My old maid will cook you something nice."

"But it's not true!" he shouted all of a sudden, and he took his head in his hands. "Nothing that I have told you is true! I've lied! I don't have a house, or a maid, or a wood, or a ship! My enemies have it all, it's all gone!"

"We will take revenge!" the children shouted vehemently. "Revenge, revenge!"

So it was that they felt full of compassion for their dear old marshal. All their games left them feeling indifferent. They didn't want to do anything except stay and chat with their old friend. But all this was too wonderful, and it couldn't last forever. One day, they went to Nina, the maid, to ask her for a snack. They liked Nina very much. She was beautiful and tanned, with a rosy complexion, and wore dainty little embroidered aprons, and she loved them very much. They went to her and asked for their snack and Nina filled the fruit dish with apricots.

"They have to be good ones, they're for the marshal," said Nennella.

"The marshal?" said Nina, in amazement.

"Yes, of course, the marshal," said the children, winking and laughing. For quite some time, they had wanted to speak about him to somebody, and Nina was so likeable.

"The marshal, what's strange about that? The marshal!" they all said together, laughing excitedly.

"Well indeed, what stories you have in your heads!" said Nina replacing the fruit bowl in the pantry. At that moment, their grandmother came in.

"What are you talking about?" she wanted to know.

"They've got a marshal," said Nina.

"What do you mean a marshal?"

"How funny they are with their stories," said Nina. "A marshal of all things! What children they are."

The children went out to the garden, carrying with them the fat apricots streaked with pink. They were no longer laughing and a sad feeling had come over them. They went down to the cellar and sat on the sofa. They waited. The evening came on. Memi took an apricot and sniffed it.

"We could eat them as well you know," he said.

"He won't come again," said Silvio, "he'll never come again. Nennella was stupid to tell. He won't play with us anymore."

"But Memi said it was all right to tell." Nennella felt very much like crying.

"He's a fool. You shouldn't believe what he says. Mamma says we shouldn't play with him, because maybe he has lice."

"It's you who have lice," said Memi. "I don't want to play with you. I'll go to the piazza and play with the older children. They play marbles, for money. I'll have fun with them."

"If you do that, you won't see the marshal," said Nennella.

"I don't care about the marshal." He said with a spiteful laugh. "There is no marshal."

"There isn't one? What do you mean there isn't one?" said Silvio, seizing him by the jumper.

"There isn't one. He doesn't exist," said Memi.

Silvio and Paolo jumped on him, and threw him to the ground. He managed to set himself free and ran out into the garden.

"There isn't one, there isn't one," he shouted, running towards the gate. "He doesn't exist! He's made up!"

The others chased him frantically. Suddenly he turned around and threw a stone. The others took two or three stones and threw them back at him.

"Stop children! You'll hurt yourselves like that!" shouted Nina the maid, who was on the grass hanging the washing. Everybody noticed what was going on, and the children were told off and punished. The cellar was closed up to prevent them going there anymore.